SUPERLATIVE SOUL
OR
NEFARIOUS SOUL

{ A Memoir }

BRENDA M. CHRISTY

Superlative Soul or Nefarious Soul

Printed by CreateSpace, 2013

Library of Congress Cataloging-in-Publication Data

Christy, Brenda M.
Superlative Soul or Nefarious Soul—First edition

Printed in the United States of America.

ISBN-10: 0989168603

ISBN-13: 978-0-9891686-0-1

DEDICATION

*God, my heavenly father, for His unconditional love for me,
and Michael M. Christy Sr., my earthly father,
for his implicit love for me.*

CONTENTS

Acknowledgments

I am indebted to my older sister, Carol Conrad, better known as "Sissie" or "Sis," for her love and encouragement. She believed in this book from day one and prayed faithfully God would sustain me throughout the writing process and that His glory would be magnified through this book.

AUTHOR'S NOTE

This book is a memoir and is drawn from actual events. The names of certain people in this book have been changed in an attempt to respect their individual privacy. Those whose names were not changed are disclosed in the book index.

PREFACE

During my upbringing, I imagined my soul as some sort of intangible, empty shell. During my journey from adolescence to adulthood, I filled this empty shell with things important to me, thereby influencing my behavior. After the murder of a coworker in 2002, I questioned the significance of my soul and where my soul would go at the time of my death. A few years passed with little change in my attitude or conduct because I was unable to let go of things I had placed enormous value on, even though I knew something larger could be gained. Ultimately, a series of ongoing adversities took hold of my life, and I experienced conviction from these hardships that helped change me and my beliefs.

One brisk day in 2012, as I was mediating on God while jogging outside, I looked down and saw a dirty leaf at my feet. I stopped and gently picked it up. I envisioned the dirty leaf as my life apart from God. The dirt on the leaf was my sinful nature, while the dryness of the leaf was my thirst to know Christ. A quote from Billy Graham helped me put the symbolism of the leaf in relation to my life into perspective: "The Bible teaches that you are an immortal soul. Your soul is eternal and will live forever...the real you—the part of you that thinks, feels, dreams, aspires;

the ego, the personality—will never die...Your soul will live forever in one of two places, heaven or hell."

Soon thereafter, I felt a nudge to share the details of my adversities and my transformation. The nudge became a push and then a shove. I started writing. I hesitated, and then I stopped. No matter how authentic my voice, I knew I would be ridiculed by my adversaries and condemned by skeptical readers. The shove knocked me down. I prayed, and then I got back on my feet. I faithfully started writing again. Seven long, distressing months passed. The final reassuring jostle to finish my memoir came when I read in God's Word from the book of Ecclesiastes: *For everything there is a season, and a time for every purpose under heaven.* **(Ecclesiastes 3:1, ASV)**

PROLOGUE

In 2002, I reported a sexual harassment complaint on behalf of a coworker. The internal investigation became a witch hunt, and my punishment for reporting the harassment was a two-day suspension and a written reprimand, while being condemned as a "whistle-blower." The results of the skewed sexual harassment investigation became a monstrosity that laid the foundation for a continuum of discriminatory and retaliatory abuse I sustained over the course of my career as a police officer. After the chief of police had previously looked me in the eyes and said to me, "You're a thorn in my side," his paintbrush smudged the canvas of my personnel file, portraying me as a futile cop, as I hopelessly watched my career aspirations being blotted out with each brush stroke.

After nearly two decades of police work under my belt, I found myself with a lump embedded in my throat as I sat in the chief's office while he read aloud a demotion letter he authored to me to justify his choreographed work of art. After I had lost my rank and a portion of my salary and exhausted all of my administrative remedies, I inevitably filed a lawsuit against my employer, the City of Myrtle Beach.

Each chapter of this memoir exposes the bricks and mortar that make up the walls of a Myrtle Beach law enforcement workplace and tells of a fractured justice system, while connecting the dots of a five-year litigation process that began with filing an official complaint with the South Carolina Human Affairs Commission, followed by motion-of-discovery demands, sworn affidavits, and sworn deposition testimonies. Throughout the duration of the agonizing legal process, I continued my career as a police officer and witnessed people, at all levels, sacrificing their souls as a survival tactic, as a masquerade, for some type of achievement or simply as a means to blame others.

In my lawsuit and throughout the latter part of my career, the deeds of many became as discernible as the black-and-white stripes of a zebra, simultaneously constructing a platform fashioned by character flaws and held together by a lack of conviction. One moral to this story is that the truth is not always your friend when you freely trade the value of your soul for nonsensical gain.

While awaiting a summary judgment decision by the United States district judge, I went through a series of difficult and painful adversities. Throughout my journey, my own sinful nature was revealed, which led me to do some solemn soul-searching that brought God's conviction, as well as His grace upon me. As my faith grew in the midst of my hardships, I had a number of ah-ha moments, one of which was identifying my soul as a gift from God that should be valued and guarded, not sacrificed. Trusting God in every circumstance is essential as the end of my law enforcement career and the outcome of my lawsuit far exceeded my greatest expectations.

1

IN THE BEGINNING

Myrtle Beach, a coastal city on the eastern shore of the United States in Horry County, South Carolina, incorporated in 1938 and became a city in 1957. It has been a top tourist destination for decades. Looking back, I wouldn't consider Myrtle Beach a big metropolitan area but rather a small town, lacking culture, as beachwear stores and tawdry billboards dotted every thoroughfare within the city limits, while banner planes polluted the skyline with "all-you-can-eat-seafood-buffet" messages. Even so, after I had spent family vacations and joined those flocking to spring breaks in Myrtle Beach, the pull of sandy shores and a warm climate had me migrating back to the region as soon as I graduated from college in 1986.

Living on my own, away from my family for the first time, felt liberating. I had intentionally put my Christian faith on hold so I wouldn't feel guilty enjoying the party scene and the new lifestyle I began living. After I took a few store-clerk and fast-food minimum-wage jobs, Dad began prodding me to get a "real job." I had become friends with a manager, Sabina, at one of the restaurants where I was working. I was six months older than Sabina, but we took the same "Thelma and Louise" approach to our adventures when exploring all that Myrtle Beach had to offer—absent any crime sprees. We became "best friends forever"; years later, I would be a bridesmaid in her wedding and soon after celebrate with her family the birth of her only child, a son. I became increasingly close to her parents, known to me as Ma and Dad Hurt. They soon placed my picture on their mantle and called me their third daughter, while offering me unlimited spiritual guidance and a seat next to them in the local church pew. My church attendance was sporadic, but Ma and Dad Hurt still faithfully prayed for God's hand upon my life.

A year had already passed since my real dad first began dropping subtle messages, and after several emotional tugs within myself, I finally decided to try to begin an occupation using the four-year degree in education I had attained as a bargaining chip. Knowing that I had never seriously pursued anything with any real ambition and with great trepidation, I spontaneously filled out an application with the Myrtle Beach Police Department to become a police officer. Weeks later, with sweaty palms and rose-colored glasses on, I walked into my first official police oral interview. Despite my college education, the hiring board members recognized the word "green" categorically stamped on my forehead but appeared to appreciate my candor and hired me as a road-patrol officer; I would be joining only a handful of other females on the police force assigned to protect the streets of

Myrtle Beach. During this time, I only remember two females who were decorated officers, holding rank within the police department: Captain Mary Grace Morgan and Lieutenant Watch Commander Rondie Peiscop-Grau. These two women were pioneers within the Myrtle Beach Police Department, and their efforts would help pave the way for me and other female officers who would later try to break the glass ceiling on top of this paramilitary organization.

The symbolic inauguration of my police career, on November 11, 1987, would be the commencement of many peaks and valleys, as well as precarious choices I would make over the next few decades, which would alter the path of my journey. When we use alacrity, absent prudence, and have a roll-the-dice approach to choices, we often create reprehensible consequences for ourselves, resulting in the skeletons we all have in our closets. Affirmation for this paradigm would come to me later, during different stages of my journey, and after reading a quote by Dr. Mary C. Neal: "Every choice we make today affects the choices that we face tomorrow."

Entering into a career field without proper knowledge of the profession was like testing the water wearing a bone-dry swimsuit and reluctantly placing my big toe in the pool only to be soaked with arctic water by a clamorous swimmer doing dolphin kicks. The beginning of my career was comparable to the much-anticipated day my training wheels were removed from my first bicycle, but with the sun in my eyes, my career path would inexorably become bumpy, producing falls, resulting in scrapes and many bruises.

To become a certified police officer, each police candidate was required to complete a multifaceted curriculum

at the criminal justice police academy in Columbia, South
Carolina. While waiting for an academy slot to become available, I worked as a jailer, a dispatcher, and at our police
department complaints-service counter, answering phones
and assisting the general public with a multitude of misfor-
tunes and inquiries. Finally, in June 1988, I began my mandatory nine weeks of training at the police academy and
successfully graduated in August of the same year. When I
started on the police force, there was no field training officer
program and no road map to follow on how to become a
good cop. I rode two nights with a skeptical road-patrol sergeant and was then turned loose to answer calls for service
in a police car on my own. My freshly polished police shoes
and heavily starched white uniform shirt had not received
the first splash of adversity yet, so I was ready to take the
plunge, headfirst—or so I thought.

When I was assigned to the Uniform Patrol Division, the
police department had approximately forty road-patrol officers, working three rotating shifts—7:00 to 3:00 p.m., 3:00 to
11:00 p.m., and 11:00 to 7:00 a.m. The city was divided into
assigned areas. Typically, there was only one officer assigned
to each area, and all areas combined blanketed approximately fourteen thousand acres and nine and a half miles of
beach. We were required to come into work fifteen minutes
prior to the beginning of our shift for a meeting known as a
"briefing." Since there was no Internet or email in the eighties, this was how we would get our area of assignments, find
out what crimes had occurred on the prior shift, have peri-
odic equipment and uniform inspections, and learn of any
new developments occurring within the department. Briefing

also gave an opportunity for impromptu bantering between the officers and planned "face time" with supervisors, which helped keep morale in an upright position. Officers assigned to a particular shift had the same days off, cultivating genuine camaraderie among shift personnel, as time off-duty was spent growing bona-fide friendships between the officers and their families.

During my career, I would work under the command of four police chiefs, with very different management styles, and it was within my first two years with the department that I would face one of a handful of beleaguering events of my career with the landfall of Hurricane Hugo just south of Myrtle Beach on September 21, 1989. As city officials and police command staff officers shared a television monitor to watch intently the trajectory of Hugo's 135 mile-per-hour winds, expert meteorologists were predicting landfall in Myrtle Beach or Charleston, South Carolina, and while Myrtle Beach officers continued to give a courageous outward appearance, in reality, there was widespread anarchy in every office and hallway inside the police department.

We put some unrehearsed provisions into place, but once then Governor Carroll Campbell Jr. gave the mandatory evacuation order, our agency was not prepared to handle the miles of congested traffic on our roadways, as residents and tourists alike waited until the last minute to make a mass exit out of the city. It soon became apparent that there was no scarcity of insular city leaders and department heads, as they failed to have the forethought to create a contingency plan to handle the destruction that a storm of this magnitude would create. I presume this was because these particular city administrators were either too young to remember or had completely forgotten the annihilation that Hurricane Hazel had brought after striking the border between North and South Carolina in 1954. And to aid the further procrastination of city officials in the configuration of a storm contingency blueprint, there were always a number of cynical veteran employees lurking in the corridors who maintained the same mindless declaration year after year: "Ain't no hurricane ever gonna hit here."

Once Hugo had passed, moving west of Charlotte, North Carolina, it was time for the police department to send officers out to assess the damage and begin to manage the thousands of city residents and sightseers congregating back in the area. The next two months proved to be a very poignant time in my career, as each officer worked mandatory twelve-hour shifts without a day off for weeks to maintain order and enforce a temporary curfew ordinance that had been put into place by the city council in an attempt to reduce looting.

Enforcing the curfew ordinance was like shooting fish in a barrel, which became tiresome. Working so many continuous days in a row caused me to forget what day of the week it was quite often. Because of the state of affairs, also fading from my memory was the euphoric punch-drunk feeling I had when I was officially sworn in as a police officer, which became troubling to me. I realized this storm could be a game-changer; I could take my ball and go home, or I could submit to the gravitational pull of public servanthood; however, Hugo would not make this an effortless decision for me.

Immediately after the storm, electricity throughout the city was out and would be indefinitely. I remember the traffic control lights were inoperable at the intersection of Oak Street and Tenth Avenue North (now known as Mr. Joe White Avenue), and I had been directing traffic for several hours without any relief. The torrential rain was drenching me like relentless waves pounding the shore, and I was cold, fatigued, and famished. As the onset of bursitis began to settle into my elbow from the constant commanding of stop and go motions to oncoming traffic, I subconsciously thought that there could not be anything worse in police work than the aftermath of a storm. Waterlogged, but not rueful, I decided to honor the vow I took during my oath of office, but unbeknownst to me, I would eventually face a version of the perfect storm in my career. The internal storm would be the beginning of career destruction for me, just as Hugo destroyed the Myrtle Beach coastline.

2

ROOKIE MISTAKES

After days off were finally reinstated and there seemed to be a sense of normalcy restored within city government, I began pursuing a degree in criminal justice at a local branch of Horry Georgetown Technical College. In class, I met my confidante, Becky Lorens. Unlike me, Becky knew her destiny was to become a cop. Becky was a smart, determined woman with a genuine heart for the well-being of others. Becky's mom, Bonnie, worked in the city manager's office of Myrtle Beach, so rather than commencing a career with the Myrtle Beach Police Department, she began her policing career with the City of Georgetown, thirty-five miles south of Myrtle Beach.

Becky and I would often stack our departments up against each other. When discussing workplace scenarios with one another, a "preexisting condition" we uncovered was men in law enforcement appeared to be threatened by women entering a field dominated by them. In the eighties, women were slowly invading territories where testosterone and egos could not sit dispassionately without voicing the opinion that women were the weaker sex and needed to be at home, cooking, cleaning, and caring for their children. Becky and I frequently found ourselves trying to find the right antidote to survive the male chauvinism virus without causing any adverse side-effects for ourselves. Sometimes, I was able to quarantine myself while working in this infectious environment, but other times, I contaminated myself when thinking out loud was perceived as me having contempt for authority.

Regrettably, sometime after our graduation, Becky was the first police officer to respond as a backup officer for what was thought to be a routine traffic stop conducted by Major Deputy Chief Spencer Guerry. Upon arrival, Becky found her comrade shot, lying in a pool of blood. Tragically, regardless of what Becky and medical professionals did to try to save his life, Major Guerry would die of his wounds two-days later. Ironically, in 1947, Major Guerry's grandfather, Berkeley County Sheriff's Deputy Warren Guerry had also been killed in the line of duty.

The suspect in Spencer Guerry's murder was apprehended within a few hours after the shooting; he was found guilty during a criminal trial and sentenced to death. Rightfully so, the suspect was executed by lethal injection in 2004, but all of this was of no relief for Becky's agony. Ultimately, she took an indefinite sabbatical leave from law enforcement. I was saddened when Becky informed me of her decision, but I continued my forward momentum, anxious to get my rookie years behind me. I looked forward to promotional opportunities as they became available.

Promotions were few and sporadic. Part of the quandary was because early on, our department did not have many police functions that were classified into specialized units, such as a SWAT team, K-9 unit, or negotiation team, so there was little room for advancement. We had an investigative division, which housed a small narcotics unit and crime-scene officers. The department also had beach-patrol officers, a traffic division, and waterfront–boulevard patrols that were titled as special operations. However, once assigned to the Uniform Patrol Division, it became difficult to advance up the career ladder because of the lack of positions within the organizational structure and because there were no promotional policies in place at that time.

Road-patrol officers often aspired to become detectives since they were seen as the cream-of-the-crop cops. Because they were perceived as extraordinary, there was an unspoken rule that road officers were not allowed to break the threshold of the door frame to the detective work bay without being accompanied by a shift supervisor. I was fascinated by the work the detectives did, and every chance I got to sneak into the detective work bay undetected, I did. I met Wade Small when he was assigned to the Investigative Division. His physical stature and deep voice made him naturally intimidating, but I instinctively stayed away from him because of his eccentric demeanor and dogmatic personality. Years later, when Small became my boss, he would brazenly call me "a thorn in his side," and before long, I would learn the hard way there was good reason for me to stay out of his sight.

In 1992, after the retirement of the chief who gave me my first crack at police work, City Manager Todd Long saw the need for change within the department, and after going through the motions of a hiring process, Long decisively placed a retired police chief from Charlotte-Mecklenburg into the driver's seat. The new chief executive officer did a lot to bring our "Mayberry" police department into the twenty-first century. He took us out of white police uniform shirts and put us into royal-blue uniforms, a universally known color to police agencies throughout the United States. He upgraded our firepower from Smith and Wesson .38 revolvers to semi-automatic firearms and also advanced our professionalism by establishing departmental policies and procedures and mounting new divisions within the department, such as the Internal Affairs Division—later known as the Office of Professional Standards.

Early on, I would trip over my shoelaces a number of times with what are usually classified as "rookie mistakes." These "mistakes" should have been inconsequential disciplinary actions but would later be overstated after the development of the "perfect storm" and after I inevitably filed a lawsuit against the City of Myrtle Beach. There was the time I went jogging on duty while assigned to patrol the former Myrtle Beach Air Force Base property. Although I was on the property I was assigned to guard and I was wearing my gun belt with my police radio turned in the on position, it was still deemed inappropriate, because I was not wearing my entire police uniform. My contention was that beach-patrol officers were permitted to swim and jog on duty as part of the requirement to stay physically fit, and I was merely taking the same opportunity to stay in shape. I lost the disputation, and a copy of the disciplinary action went into my personnel file.

There was another time I was disciplined after driving a police car out of town to attend the funeral of a former colleague who had committed suicide using his own service revolver. While out of town, the police car broke down and had to be towed by a wrecker service back to Myrtle Beach. Still mourning the loss of a good cop and close friend, I took a belligerent attitude when questioned by superiors about the mechanical failure of the police car. Although my superiors found no violation of protocol, I received a write-up for my argumentative demeanor.

Momentarily fast-forwarding to when Wade Small called me "a thorn in his side" and I eventually filed a lawsuit, Small later provided the following information in a sworn affidavit prepared for the court:

From 1985 to December 1992, I served in the capacity of an investigator. From 1985 until approximately August 1992, I was assigned to Investigations. I had little contact with Officer Christy during that time frame...

Small goes on to assert:

In August 1992, I was reassigned to the newly formed Administrative Division under Police Chief S. Kilson, and assigned to Internal Affairs and Policy Development. During my time in the Administrative Division (August 1992 through November 1993), my contact with Officer Christy was minimal.

As stated, Small acknowledged that he had had little contact with me from 1985 through 1992, which included the first five years of my career and minimal contact with me in 1993 but somehow found it compulsory to include the "jogging out of uniform" and "mechanical failure of a police car" as part of his colorful affidavit narrative, despite the fact the documented discipline was created by other people during that time. I would later have a hard time understanding how corrective action that occurred in 1993 would be relevant to Small's repeated refusal to promote me to the rank of sergeant after he became my boss in 1997 and ultimately his decision to demote me in 2007.

Admittedly, there were times I had a hard time keeping my vocal cords in check as my mouth was often at full throttle, resulting in brain overload. I recall an incident where I used a couple of explicit words when ordering a firefighter lieutenant to move his fire engine out of the way of a traffic collision that I had responded to assist with. The outcome of the inquiry into this incident was predictable, and I would have to fall on my sword defending my position once the corrective action was administered. In retrospect, I believe that these "rookie mistakes" had occurred because I was ignoring essential scriptures, such as: *My dear brothers, take note of this: Everyone should be quick to listen, slow to speak and slow to become angry.* **(James 1:19, NIV)** I was also of the opinion that the male-dominated police department was still adapting to the inclusion of women.

Not all of the corrective action I received had that awful medicine aftertaste as anticipated. There was the time when one of the officers on my shift began chasing a car operated by a suspected drunk driver. The intoxicated driver bailed out of the car and darted into the darkness of the night. The suspect was believed to have run into a breezeway of a local barbershop, and all the officers on shift saturated the area. I eased my police car up to the barbershop and turned my headlights off as I came around the backside of the building. I glanced into the breezeway, and all of a sudden, I collided head-on with another police car coming from the opposite side of the building. This was one time I was glad that police cars had not yet been equipped with in-car cameras and relieved to learn there was no video surveillance footage of the barbershop parking lot to capture my embarrassing predicament. Though no one was hurt in the collision and the suspect was never apprehended, damage to both police cars was substantial.

The officer driving the other police car, Billy Gilray, was fuming mad at me, and smoke rolled out from his ears when he heard news of the "Keystone cops'" head-on collision went through the police department like a runaway horse. Billy and I became the brunt of many jokes in briefing and a topic of conversation around the command staff water cooler, but the collision became comical when Billy was nicknamed "Bumper" by all the officers. Soon thereafter, Billy proudly owned the nickname, and years later, as I attended Billy's funeral, I willfully cracked a grin at the grave site when I overheard officers reflecting on Billy's admirable police career while referring to him as "Bumper."

After work one warm summer night, a spirit of gratitude fell upon me as I drove home. As I gazed into a star-filled sky looking through my windshield, I couldn't help but believe that God had orchestrated my new calling as a police officer. I paused and concluded that some of the dilemmas I was involved in were hilarious; in hindsight, I realize my nemesis through the difficult years of my career was my resistance to allowing God to have authority over my life. I had placed God on a shelf because following God required that I give up a life to gain a life. Throughout most of my police career, I simply wasn't ready to give up the life I was living for the life God had for me. Yet, after I conceded to some of these rookie mistakes, God showed His favor upon me, and I began digging myself out of the hole I was in to have some measureable levels of success.

In the middle 1990s, community policing became the flavor of the month, as all police agencies were looking for ways to gain public trust and bridge the gap between police and citizens. The department began a two-officer bicycle patrol pilot program, and I was selected as one of the officers for this patrol. The bicycle patrol was a success within a short time, as it expanded by leaps and bounds, and I was promoted to supervise the newly formed unit. During the same time frame, I humbly shared the podium with Corporal Dustin Furrier when we both won the 1994 Police Officer of the Year award during a Rotary Club luncheon, but change would soon be on the horizon for me as well as for the department.

Five years into his tour of duty, Chief Kilson unexpectedly threw in the towel to spend more time with his family. City Manager Long would then extend his pointer finger internally to Wade Small. Officers hoped that the newly appointed Chief Small would follow in the footsteps of the departing chief and continue creating a more enviable work environment. Instead, Small, as a department head, was a yes-man for memoranda being circulated from City Hall, and he soon developed a reputation as a micromanaging police chief, who had to have his fingerprints on everything within the department.

With a few years of supervision under my belt, I was recruited by then Captain of Investigations Sal Helman to transfer into the narcotics unit as the unit supervisor. He promised me a brand-new, take-home sports car for my undercover work, a clothing allowance, and the opportunity to work a flexible schedule. I jumped at the chance to work in a plainclothes undercover capacity, and three years into my narcotics assignment, I was promoted to the rank of detective. Once I moved into my assigned desk within the Investigative Division, my future appeared sunny, without a rain cloud in sight. But an unpredicted weather pattern was about to surface, one which would turn the forecast dark and dreary, as I was unknowingly headed into the center of a volatile storm. It was the "perfect storm."

3

THE PERFECT STORM

The city experienced significant growth over the next several years, and true to form, growing pains would follow. The city as a whole created several new positions to handle the increasing public service demands created by an influx of tourists during the summer season and a number of retirees making Myrtle Beach their new residence. The police department was bursting at the seams and could no longer comfortably house all the police personnel within the one-story, brick law enforcement building, which was later named after a former longtime city court judge, Ted C. Collins. At the time I was promoted to the rank of detective, the city was in the process of purchasing and leasing land to construct and renovate buildings in order to create space for all the additional personnel.

Once real estate was acquired, the police department followed suit and created a police substation and police annex station. To ease overcrowding, the Investigative Division and other specialized units were then moved into these two buildings. For the Investigative Division, the move into the police annex, located on the former Myrtle Beach Air Force Base property, had both advantages and pitfalls. One of the pitfalls of not having office space at the main police department was that the gatekeeper, tasked with overseeing daily operations, stayed at the main police department, which allowed some of the detectives to take an indefinite recess from work while wreaking havoc on certain coworkers.

Detectives were responsible for investigating a wide variety of crimes ranging from petty theft to robbery to homicide. Before the perfect storm hit, I took great pleasure in working as a detective. Unlike a patrol officer, whose primary responsibility is to gather and report pertinent facts related to a specific crime, a detective was responsible for following up on leads to solve the case and oftentimes, developing probable cause to arrest the perpetrator. I enjoyed the autonomy that came with being a detective and frequently used my position to be a victim's advocate for persons who had ill-fated encounters with wicked opportunists.

The atmosphere of the Investigative Division was created within one oversized room consisting of twelve desks with no partitions or dividers to form individual cubicles. Nine male detectives and three female detectives occupied those desks. The average age of this chosen group of men and women was approximately thirty-four, with an average of eight years of law enforcement experience. The majority of these detectives had attained bachelor's degrees, and many had attended other advanced and specialized schools and training. Because of the close working quarters and the necessity for detectives to assist each other on crime scenes and in working complex cases, we all knew each other's personalities and work ethics. Cohesiveness among the group was imperative, and rocking the boat would prove costly when supervisors completed employee evaluations or made recommendations for promotion.

Donna McFarland was a charming female detective, but she had a whimsical personality. She was always known to go with the majority opinion, regardless of the topic. Troy Akel was a male detective who was notorious for instigating controversy among the detectives. He was seen by the others as a "playground bully." Donna's inadvertent doormat semblance made her a target for Troy when he began directing a lengthy series of flagrant, sexually charged verbal and nonverbal assaults upon her in the presence of me and other coworkers. Donna would often pretend not to notice the inappropriate behaviors while some of Troy's office pals would chuckle at her attempt to hide her discomfort. I saw the absurdity in Troy's actions, but I assumed Donna would reach her threshold of tolerance and eventually follow departmental protocol to report the violations.

Troy's unwelcome gestures and language continued for some time until Donna expressed her disapproval to her friend and confidant, Detective Kevin Gibbons. Kevin would eventually inform our immediate supervisor, Detective Sergeant James Kalis, but the complaint fell on deaf ears. I would later hear firsthand from Donna that she complained about Troy's inappropriate conduct to at least three other coworkers before approaching me. Donna complained to me that Troy's harassment toward her had taken place over the

course of a year and graduated to unwanted physical touching. Donna painfully described to me an encounter where
Troy grabbed her around her waistline while at the police
annex during normal shift hours. Despite Donna's repeated
orders for Troy to let go of her, she stated her freedom did
not come immediately and Troy's behavior often made her
physically sick.

Donna advised me she had informed her four adult children of her current work dilemma, which she felt later proved
to be a mistake, as the information created discontent within
her immediate family. Her children sternly warned her she
had better report the harassment or they would. Donna said
she told her children that she would take care of it and then
finally told me the details because she knew I had "big ova-
ries." That Donna did not have the backbone to file her own
complaint was perplexing to me; I'm assuming Donna told
me because she knew that I would not play possum after
hearing firsthand of the debauchery.

What Donna originally told me about could be a criminal matter, according to the State of South Carolina code of
laws, and at the time, all of the consequences of reporting
this were not apparent to me. Donna's description of events
left me no choice with regard to city policy, and in February
2002, I filed a sexual harassment complaint on behalf of
Donna with Lieutenant Carl Chamberlain. As the perfect
storm blew ashore in a whirlwind, a bizarre turn of events
occurred when Chief Small directed our immediate supervisors in the Investigative Division to conduct an internal
investigation as opposed to having ranking officials within

our Internal Affairs Office of Professional Standards Division conduct the interviews utilizing tape recorders.

Using tape recorders during the interview process had always been standard procedure, based on the seriousness of the complaint. It was obvious to me from the beginning of the investigation that Chief Small was not going to receive the truth but rather a watered-down version that could later be misconstrued and "written off." A less-than-lethal account could then be presented to the city manager, a version that would not reflect poorly on Chief Small, since his title ultimately left him responsible for all divisions within the police department.

As the investigation took shape, it was like Moses parting the Red Sea; the opinions among the detectives were split. Half of the detectives expressed that they were relieved the situation was out in the open and was going to be dealt with, while the other half of the group took Troy's side, stating the complaint was not plausible because Donna "hears voices" and has "snakes in her head." At the onset of the inquiry, each detective was required to write a special report detailing any incidents he or she might recall. Each detective was then interviewed, often multiple times, as the investigation continued for months. As the questioning proceeded, it became a witch hunt instead of a legitimate fact-finding inquiry. During the mayhem, I was ordered to write out what I felt would be a suitable punishment for Troy. To me, this was an inappropriate order, and my only response was that I wanted to have an amicable work environment for all of us, as it was not my place to decide or administer corrective action.

As the goat rope continued, Donna advised me that she had been called into the office of the current Captain of Investigations, Bob Franklin. During the meeting, Bob began to interrogate Donna about a death investigation from 2001, in which she was the lead detective. The family of the deceased had filed a lawsuit against the city, and Franklin used this detail as leverage to help persuade Donna to renounce the sexual harassment complaint. After her meeting, Donna walked out to the back entrance of the police annex, at which time she used the opportunity to tell me she thought we were both going to be fired and she just wanted things to "be normal again." I had no idea from Donna's camouflaged advisement that she was going to throw me under the bus. I also didn't believe once a sexual harassment complaint was filed that it could be swept under the carpet, but hours later, I learned Donna had recanted her allegations through our chain of command and advised them that I had manufactured the sexual harassment complaint she provided to me, possibly to take the microscope lens off my own potentially flawed work performance.

I became the scapegoat of the perfect storm when Chief Small gave me a two-day suspension without pay and a written reprimand for reporting the sexual harassment. Due to the seriousness of the disciplinary action, I was removed from the existing sergeant's promotional pool, despite the fact I had placed third on the list of seven other candidates. I was later told by a constituent that "no good deed goes unpunished."

As the weeks went on, my assigned caseload notably increased to the point I struggled to complete it. This obviously reaffirmed in my mind that they were retaliating against me for filing the sexual harassment complaint. At the end of April 2002, I requested a transfer out of the Investigative Division. Chief Small immediately granted the request and took the liberty to assign me as a midnight-shift supervisor. Out of all areas of assignment, midnight shift was one of the least desirable, primarily because of the night-shift working hours.

By July 2002, Donna was promoted to administrative sergeant of the Internal Affairs Office of Professional Standards, a position with limited supervisory responsibilities, and within the same year, Troy was also promoted to sergeant. In August 2004, Donna was once again promoted, this time to the rank of administrative lieutenant, continuing her assignment in the Internal Affairs Office of Professional Standards Division. Obtaining two promotions in such a short time was almost unheard of, but Donna's career advancements would suggest that some women in the department were being promoted to cover up harassment and discrimination complaints and provide statistical evidence to use against future grievances.

At the end of the day, I believe Donna sacrificed her soul at my expense. *And how do you benefit if you gain the whole world but lose your own soul in the process? Is anything worth more than your soul?* **(Mark 8:36–37, NLT)** After the fallout, those on the outside looking in and those on the inside who knew of Donna's capricious behavior asked me the million-dollar question: "Why did you go to bat for Donna?" My two-prong summarization was "One, city policy, and two, to keep from sacrificing my soul by taking the same 'bury your head in the sand' approach the others had chosen."

The perfect storm would be the beginning of my career taking a downhill spiral. Years later, I would file an unavoidable lawsuit on my behalf. After the lawsuit was filed, Donna would inescapably be subpoenaed for a sworn deposition. Excerpts from Donna's testimony, under oath, exposed her pseudo-amnesia disorder at the time she recanted her recollection of these events to our superiors in 2002, and this occurred again when she was questioned during her deposition in 2010.

Q: And who was the person who made you feel uncomfortable?

A: Troy Akel.

Q: Okay. What were the things that were done that made you uncomfortable?

A: The eye movement, looking up and down.

Q: Up and down on?

A: Looking at me. The interference when I was on the telephone of gyrating around my chair, pushing my chair around.

Q: Was he...

A: I prefer to forget that. It's not a very comfortable memory there, so...

Q: So it did make you uncomfortable?

A: Yes. It was an uncomfortable period of time, yes.

Q: Was there any touching involved?

A: I think he may have touched my chair when I was sitting in it and twisted it back and forth, so I can't recall if he did or did not physically touch me. He may have; I don't know. But it wasn't intrusive touching as far as groping or anything like that.

Q: Did he approach you in a way that was too close for comfort?

A: Yes.

Q: Was there ever an incident that occurred in a kitchen that made you uncomfortable? In a kitchen at work?
A: No, the incidents that I remember were in the office. And in the hallway.
Q: In the hallway, what happened in the hallway?
A: The up-and-down eyes, "What's for breakfast this morning?" or whatever. Some kind of comment like that.
Q: Was there any proposition?
A: No, I don't recall that.
Q: Any sexual remarks to you?
A: There was some, yes. Some joking. I don't recall particulars and specifics what it was.
Q: Did it make you uncomfortable?
A: Yes.
Q: Did you speak to Brenda Christy about your discomfort?
A: Yes.
Q: And did you express that you were displeased with what was going on?
A: Yes.

Even though Donna never mustered up the three words that I desperately wanted to hear, "I'm sorry, Brenda," she appeared contrite as she cried during this part of her deposition. As I watched Donna squirm in her chair, I thought to myself, *Did she just say what I thought she said?* I then took into account that Chief Small and others with leading influence over Donna were not in the deposition room to hold her hand or pull her puppet strings in order for her to provide scripted answers. Although Donna's murky confession did not provide details of the criminal aspects of the sexual harassment or the duration of these events, it was still a miraculous phenomenon for me to hear, finally, eight years after I had reported the harassment on her behalf.

As I watched Donna testify, I placed my hand over my mouth and began grinding my teeth to keep from shouting out, Hallelujah! Hallelujah!

When in the court of law, before testifying, we take an oath to tell the truth, the whole truth, and nothing but the truth. After Donna's deposition, it was my prayer that when we all finally took our seats in a federal courtroom and Donna placed her hand on the Bible, she would be convicted to inform the judge and jurors explicitly of the sexual harassment she endured, which in itself would expose what city officials had covered up.

4

OFFICER DOWN

But when the Holy Spirit controls our lives, he will produce this kind of fruit in us: love, joy, peace, patience, kindness, goodness, faithfulness, gentleness and self-control. Here there is no conflict with the law.
(Galatians 5:22–23, NLT)

In late spring 2002, I assumed my duties as a midnight-shift patrol supervisor under the direction of Sergeant Dave Bridgmon and Sergeant Harvey Raines. Dave would subsequently retire, leaving Harvey and me to oversee a dozen or more road-patrol officers on shift. I enjoyed working for Harvey, as he made me think of a good-guy cartoon action figure with a charismatic personality and an invisible cape draped over his uniform. Harvey and I developed a good rapport as we worked closely together for the next few years. Eight months into my assignment on midnight shift, we would face an unexpected tragedy, and it would be our strong work alliance and faith in Christ that would bring us through the devastating events of December 29, 2002.

Just four days after Christmas, I dismissed my officers from briefing into a chilly winter night for what should have been a slow, routine patrol shift. As I was still echoing the holiday Yuletide cheer and sanguinity, I hung around the office and began sorting through a stack of hand-me-down assignments that had been pushed off the desk of Patrol Lieutenant Chuck Davis and neatly stacked into a pile with a Post-It note that read, "Inv. Christy." Chuck had been named by those receiving his delegated assignments as "Pass the Buck Chuck" because he routinely used proverbial paper shuffling as a decoy for his adeptness in taking credit for the work completed by others. I began mapping out the to-do list as the second hand on the wall clock at the complaints-service counter rested on the bottom of the hour, indicating thirty minutes past midnight.

Seconds later, my multitasking was abruptly interrupted by screams of panic as officers inadvertently interrupted each other over the police radio to report shots had been fired at a local doughnut-coffee shop, just nineteen blocks from the police department. I jumped into a police car with Sergeant Judy Harris. Judy barreled out of the police department parking lot as I operated the blue lights and siren buttons and informed police dispatchers that we were responding. As we sped up Oak Street, I had no idea that anyone had been shot. Judy and I desperately tried to assess the situation from the pandemonium we were hearing over the police radio.

I would have to rely on my experience from the Investigative Division, as I had been previously involved in diverse death investigations, from suicides and traffic fatalities to hospice deaths and homicides, but nothing could prepare me for what I would witness when I arrived at the incident location.

After coming to a screeching halt, Judy and I left the police car in the middle of the road on Kings Highway and quickly joined the officers already on scene. Officer Mark Geyer briefed me that Officer 263 had been shot. Mark said he then returned fire and became involved in a gun battle with the suspect. With guns drawn, we were now in a stand-off with the suspect as we tried to anticipate his next move. Moments later, the suspect fled the scene in a compact car driven by a female accomplice.

Mark, Officer Natalie Potton, and I then ran to help the officer who had been shot while other officers pursued the fleeing suspects. Mark and Natalie immediately began administering CPR while I hovered over them, as I was unable to do any more than what Mark and Natalie were already doing to aid the wounded officer. I was in disbelief that the officer shot was wearing the same blue uniform that I was wearing. It was inconceivable to me that anyone would shoot a police officer.

While standing over Officer 263, I recalled that he was always full of the Fruits of the Spirit (*love, joy, peace, patience, kindness, goodness, faithfulness, gentleness, and self-control*), and he was truly an angel disguised in a police uniform. As I exhaled repeatedly into the frigid air, I watched my breath rise and disappear. When I looked at this valiant officer's lifeless body, I had no doubt that his soul had already risen from him, preordained for heaven, just as my breath vanished instantaneously. In my anguish, I told Mark and Natalie in an urgent tone, "We need to pray right now!" Both Mark and Natalie, aghast, then gave me a penetrating look while frantically continuing CPR.

As the doughnut-coffee shop parking lot was now a murder scene, Harvey desperately rifled through the trunk of his police car and pulled out a roll of yellow "POLICE LINE DO NOT CROSS" tape and swiftly forced one end of the tape into my hand like a relay runner handing off a baton. I began running the tape around the perimeters of the parking lot to rope off the entire area but felt as if I were running on shifting sand. I was running as fast as I possibly could but didn't feel like I was going anywhere as a dubious spirit weighed me down. As I continued running to mark off the vicinity, the question, *Why did God allow this horrific tragedy to happen?* raced through my mind. I rounded the corner of the parking lot, and I could see the anxious look on Harvey's face as he stared at me intently trying to somehow make my feet move faster.

Within minutes after securing the crime scene, we learned that the suspect's vehicle had been stopped just a few miles away by police stop stick strips, and both suspects had been taken into police custody. Chief Small arrived at the doughnut-coffee shop and approached me as I sat in the front seat of a crime scene van, relinquishing evidence to a crime scene supervisor. "Are you okay?" Small asked.

Without hesitation, I said, "No, I'm not." Even though I had been exposed to many death investigations as a detective,

I wasn't trained to separate myself from the death of an officer, and at the time of this tragedy, the department had no specialized training in place for line-of-duty deaths.

I consciously thought of what my friend Becky had told me about how she felt after witnessing the murder of a fallen hero, Spencer Guerry, in Georgetown, South Carolina, just eight years earlier. The troubling realization that witnessing the murder of a fellow officer would now mean an unwanted, wretched common thread sewn into the tapestry of the law enforcement careers of my confidante Becky and me, created a numbing, sickening feeling in the pit of my stomach. I would later share the details of what I experienced with Becky and her husband as Becky and I grieved over the commonalities of these tragedies and the continued guilt we suffered for not being able to prevent them.

The following day, I had a debriefing counseling session with the city's mental health analyst, Dr. Elbert Rouselle, who also maintained a private practice specializing in marriage counseling. I had a tremendous amount of remorse surrounding the death of Officer 263, and it was apparent to me after my initial debriefing and my follow-up session with Dr. Rouselle that I would need to seek therapy from a psychologist specializing in trauma and aftermath recovery. When I called Dad and my stepmom, Linda, and then conversed with my siblings, everyone was adamant that I should come home to West Virginia where I could receive support from my loving family and specialized treatment from a therapist. I immediately began counseling sessions with Dr. Neve Sagucio in Morgantown, West Virginia. After an initial counseling session and assessment, Dr. Sagucio sent a written diagnosis and treatment plan to Dr. Rouselle and Chief Small:

Following being present at the fatal shooting of a fellow officer four days ago, this female detective is experiencing symptoms of acute stress disorder (including depersonalization, sleep interruption, poor concentration, hyper-vigilance, and emotional lability) when encountering any activities, apparel, or thoughts of returning to work. She is intelligent, has a strong family and social support group, and is compliant with therapy. She is hoping to be able to return to her duties and thus is seeking counseling as soon as possible following recognition that her reactions are dysfunctional. Provisionally, it appears as though this client is going to be able to recover quickly and thoroughly providing she continues to be offered support from those in her home and community, and voluntarily seeks counseling. Her triggers seem to surround her job, so therapy offered through the department for which she works seems to be a secondary trigger, and therefore counter-therapeutic. The goal of therapy is to eventually regain a sense of independence. Number of sessions needed range anywhere from 4–10 sessions, temporally spaced closer together at first, and then gradually phasing out the need for therapist intervention as the techniques and skills learned are put into action in her own home, and job.

I returned to Myrtle Beach approximately two weeks later and had a concluding session with Dr. Rouselle at which time I was released to full duty status and returned to work. As part of my healing process, I took it upon myself to become knowledgeable of the stories of Lieutenant John Ronald Floyd, Sergeant Henry O'Dell Stalvey Jr., Corporal Dennis James Lyden, and Lieutenant Randy Gene Gerald, all local police officers who had also been killed in the line of duty. The tragic events took place just prior to me becoming a cop and sadly continued throughout some stage of my law enforcement career. For me, these officers' unfortunate deaths raised the level of awareness of the hazards to the men and women serving in the public safety profession, an awareness that I unintentionally did not have until I witnessed this fatal incident.

This tragedy left me with an **ah-ha moment:** Life can stop on a dime. As scripture warns us: *How do you know what will happen tomorrow? For your life is like the morning fog— it's here a little while, then it's gone.* **(James 4:14, NLT)** Life on earth has an expiration date. This knowledge caused me to consciously consider what would have happened if I had been killed instead of Officer 263. I then asked myself a difficult question: *Where would my soul go if I were to die today?* I incorrectly thought that I had purchased enough fire insurance when I had previously proclaimed: *For God so loved the world that he gave his one and only son, that whoever believes in him shall not perish but have eternal life.* **(John 3:16, NIV)** But more than just believing John 3:16, I would ultimately realize that I needed to come to terms with repentance and turn from my sinful nature to secure my soul in eternity.

In death, and with other significant occurrences throughout our journey, we often look for a silver lining. Death symbolizes the end of the journey, but through the untimely passing of Myrtle Beach Officer 263, an illuminating light was cast on the death of the first Myrtle Beach police officer killed in the line of duty, Officer Henry Howard Scarborough.

Officer Scarborough was shot and killed on March 7, 1949, his very first day of duty. Another officer returned fire, wounding Scarborough's assailant, who later died from his injuries. Unfortunately, there was no financial compensation for the families of officers killed in the line of duty at that time, but upon learning of Officer Scarborough's death, the Myrtle Beach community and business owners pulled together to raise six thousand dollars for his family. A public luncheon was then held to honor Officer Scarborough's life and sacrifice, while helping to provide proper closure for his surviving family members some fifty-seven years later. Although these heroic officers have passed, their contributions to humanity will not be forgotten. And appropriately, each year, a memorial service is held to mark the anniversary of the death of Officer 263.

The memorial service is often led by Chief Small and organized by the command staff and the police department's Honor Guard. It helps to give comfort to grieving family members and officers who are still mourning. Suitably, the scripture inscribed on the police department monument for Officer 263 is: *Blessed are the peacemakers: for they shall be called the children of God.* **(Matthew 5:9, KJV)** Unfortunately, I would involuntarily relive the anguish I still held from witnessing this heartbreak when I read an excerpt from a sworn affidavit that had been later provided to the court and written by Donna McFarland, which made reference to me and this tragic event.

> I was promoted out of Investigations sometime in 2002. In December 2002, Officer Joe McGarry was shot and killed. Christy was on the scene and I remember she was out of work for some time after that because she said she was having a hard time dealing with it. I saw her in the hallway sometime after, and she conveyed to me that she had been out of work because of it.

Chief Small also made a similar reference to me leaving town "to visit my family" after the death of Officer 263 in his sworn affidavit. Both statements by Donna McFarland and Chief Small were then used by the city's legal defense team in their attempt to disprove the basis of my lawsuit, which notably was filed seven years after this fatal incident and was absolutely unrelated to this officer's death. It was immoral of Donna McFarland and Chief Small to bring up this officer's death to somehow reflect negatively on me given the fact this information had no evidentiary value concerning my claims of discrimination and retaliation. And unfortunately, throughout my lawsuit proceedings, I would persistently experience more appalling tactics of this nature.

5

PANDORA'S BOX

After several months of being on midnight shift, I adjusted to being up all night while normal folks slept. I learned how to catnap throughout the day until it was time to go back into work, but before the newness of being a midnight shift supervisor wore off, Chief Small would "shake things up." It was well known that prior to spring break and the height of our peak summer tourist season, the chief would move supervisors and officers to different divisions and shifts twice a year. Small believed in diversity among his officers and supervisors, and part of his philosophy was that officers and supervisors should be well-rounded enough to work any area within the department over the course of their career. This forced reluctant supervisors to have diversified in-house portfolios, as well as created an opportune time to address any dysfunction among shift members and grant any officer transfer requests.

The cycle would again repeat itself with more personnel swaps shortly after Labor Day weekend, when the slower winter golf season would get underway. During one of these transitional periods, Harvey and I were named with a host of others to be moved, and we would eventually land together as day-shift patrol supervisors. This would be an important fact, as the chief and his command staff would later contend in their sworn affidavits I caused problems and had to be moved around from one unit to another. This statement was one of several misrepresentations of facts presented to the court by the city's legal defense team that I would need to dispute at a later time.

While supervising day-shift patrol, I competed in the 2004 to 2005 sergeant promotional process. After testing, the chief posted the candidate rankings by memorandum, which showed me sandwiched in between the top contender, Investigator Fred Hill, and the number-three candidate, Investigator Greg Kaufman. In addition to my placement in the sergeant promotional pool, I received a "substantially exceeds expectation" rating on my employee performance evaluation. Harvey's written comments on the evaluation were, "Brenda has finally arrived at the pinnacle, and she is currently in the top three, awaiting promotion."

Uniform Patrol Captain Jerry Veit also gave his stamp of approval when he concurred with my evaluation and wrote, "I'm in hopes she keeps this up and gets promoted in the process." However, the timing of disturbing information would cause another black cloud to form directly over my head.

Overseeing day-shift patrol one afternoon, Patrol Officer Kaleb Lang came to me with distressing news. Kaleb informed me that Troy Akel had a group photograph of the detective division personnel hanging on the wall above his desk. Kaleb said that there was a piece of black electrical tape covering my face, and he was embarrassed for me when assuming I was unaware of Troy's "trophy" picture. Troy's desk was in the detective work bay, which was an open common area of the police department annex where numerous personnel walked through on a regular basis.

One Sunday afternoon, while calls for service were low, I went to the detective work bay and saw the framed picture that had black tape over my face. I was humiliated and in disbelief that a group photograph with a hostile overtone was permitted to be on display.

I immediately sent a memorandum to Chief Small through Harvey and the rest of my chain of command, requesting that the photograph Troy placed on exhibit be removed. Still reeling from the sexual harassment complaint I filed, Chief Small fired back by ordering disciplinary action taken against me for going into the detective work bay on "unofficial" business.

Feeling as if my Achilles' tendon had just been slashed with a razor, I limped into the office of a coworker, simultaneously dragging my chin on the floor. The coworker suggested that I speak with his attorney, Paul Marshal. Weeks later, I reluctantly went to Marshal's law office for a consultation. Marshal's jaw dropped as I explained the sequence of events that had transpired, and when I advised him of the succession of disciplinary action I received after reporting sexual harassment and for complaining about the taped-up photograph, his eyes enlarged, and he began to salivate.

This foaming-at-the-mouth approach by Marshal to file a lawsuit against the city caused me to reconsider my years of devoted service to the department. Against Marshal's expressed counsel, I quietly slipped back into the rank and file at the police department and tried to stay off of Chief Small's radar. I remember praying with Ma and Dad Hurt and asking for God's help, guidance, and protection. However, I was still not ready to fully relinquish my life for the plan God had for me.

Day-shift patrol stayed consistently busy, and each patrol shift endured manpower deficiencies similar to the Red Cross suffering from a critical blood supply shortage. In an attempt to stop the hemorrhaging, the command staff would continually cancel days off throughout the summer months to beef up patrol coverage. This created a revolving-door syndrome at the infamous north door of the police department for officers turning in their police badges in search of a profession offering a better quality of life. Needless to say, the turnover rate of the department was evident.

During one of those busy day shifts, where I had just enough officers to cover the mandatory areas of assignment, I received information about a guy wanted for credit-card fraud who was supposedly working at an area motel on the south-end of Ocean Boulevard. I was responding to the motel from the north-end city limits when I instructed Patrol Officer Jake Faulkner to respond to the motel. Jake was a field training officer, who had grown up in a rural area of Horry County and had been nicknamed "Big Country" for his big build and laid-back personality.

At the time, I knew Jake had a new officer riding with him who had prior experience as a probation, parole, and pardon agent. I felt comfortable that Jake and his partner could handle the situation if they arrived before me. Jake called my cell phone and advised me that the field training officer's manual specified new officers could not be utilized as a backup officer in certain situations. I pulled rank on Jake and informed him that the FTO manual was just a guideline and not departmental regulation. I then reiterated my command for Jake and his partner to respond to the motel. As I predicated, once Jake and his partner arrived at the motel, no specialized show of force, such as a SWAT team or a state law enforcement police helicopter, was needed. The suspect was located, arrested, and brought to jail.

I thought the chess match was over until Jake told another supervisor that I made him violate FTO guidelines. The supervisor then opened up Pandora's box when she scampered up to Lieutenant Donna McFarland's office to play "tattletales." Armed with what McFarland perceived as incriminating information, she sent out an email to all police personnel, implying that my choice for handling the fugitive was inappropriate and FTO guidelines would be strictly adhered to. When I read McFarland's email, it was like ripping off a Band-Aid without warning. I was annoyed, and as with some of the previous interpersonal communication mistakes I've made, I took a swift, deliberate, ear-piercing approach when confronting Jake with McFarland's email. Office gossipers with no eyewitness account of my admonition to Jake would put their own seasoning on the steak by describing me as a spinning-out-of-control Tasmanian devil in a temper tantrum.

God's Word reads, *If you claim to be religious but don't control your tongue, you are just fooling yourself, and your religion is worthless.* **(James 1:26, NLT)** Convicted by scripture and on my own accord, I apologized to Jake and continued to supervise him and the other officers on shift, without any additional drama, until weeks later when word of the ordeal crept into the command staff hallway known by the officers as "Mahogany Row."

The command staff hallway was depicted by officers as Mahogany Row because of the hefty, oversized wooden desks these appointed police executives occupied, and for good reason, Mahogany Row was normally not a place officers wanted to loiter. I had knowledge that my name wasn't the only supervisor's name that had been batted around on Mahogany Row. Max Malone was a corporal with a history of tyrannical, belittling yelling episodes that kept discord among his subordinates. Max would habitually terrorize his officers and then relish when one would quit or beg for a transfer from under his command. The subordinates who complained were made out to be crybabies, and Max's behavior was downplayed by the command staff as him being "a little rough around the edges."

The ink was barely dry on the last reprimand I was given for complaining about the black-tape photograph, and now Chief Small was once again contemplating punishment against me for my word exchange with Jake. In November 2004, Chief Small removed me as a day-shift supervisor and ordered me to complete a six-month ride-along with Sergeant Mickey Burke for ten hours a week. Additionally, I received a written reprimand and was reassigned to the warrant unit.

I witnessed firsthand an unspoken "thin-blue-line subculture" that exists in police work, a double standard concerning males and females carrying out the same supervisory role. Although the rank carries the same responsibility for men and women, it is acceptable for a male superior to yell and use subordinates as verbal punching bags without repercussion. This behavior is seen as "just part of the job." However, if an order or reprimand given by a female superior is perceived as too harsh of a tongue-lashing, it is almost always met with opposition and contested up the chain of command by the male subordinate.

By this time, I had already received an unprecedented amount of disciplinary action from Chief Small and the severity was more than all three previous police chiefs' pens combined. I felt like I had been beaten down by the discipline more than a piñata at a kindergarten birthday party, and it was clear Chief Small still had more ink to use.

6

MARCHING ORDERS

fter receiving my marching orders, I reported to the warrant unit and the mandatory ride-along program for my six-month period that would seem like a six-month prison sentence in Alcatraz. I met with my new boss, Sergeant Hubert Keith. Hubert was a very tall, lanky, humble African American, whose outward appearance alone could make him pass for a prison warden. Hubert took pride when wearing his police uniform and in his devoted service to his church and the community. Hubert started his career with the Myrtle Beach Police Department in 1965, when the annual police salary was stuck around six thousand dollars and it was still acceptable to use the "N" word when describing a person's race. Hubert welcomed me with open arms to assist him working warrants and took me under his wing. He became my mentor and one of my best friends in the department.

Since the police department did not have any officers working warrants on a full-time basis until then, the clerk of courts office had a backlog of active arrest warrants. After taking the time to physically hand count 2,549 outstanding arrest warrants, finding a way to streamline and expedite warrant service took on an urgent precedence. However, I was still required to complete a weekly ten-hour ride-along with Sergeant Mickey Burke. Mickey had a reputation for being a frugal, eBay guru who was always on the hunt for a bargain. I was an unwilling passenger in Mickey's police car when he would be on a shopping expedition trying to find the best price on vehicle tires for his brother or paying for a load of fill dirt he had delivered at his newly constructed house.

Mickey never gave me the opportunity to have any interaction with his shift personnel; therefore, in retrospect, it would have been hard for him to give me a pass or fail grade in my newly assigned position. To my knowledge, Mickey did not complete any daily observational reports concerning our time with each other because he never provided me with any feedback for the ride-alongs we completed together. Mickey would later claim as part of the lawsuit proceedings that I failed this ride-along program and was unworthy to be promoted to sergeant. Unfortunately, the only influence Mickey had on me for the duration of time I rode with him would be learning that using the Sunday newspaper coupon section could be an effective cost-cutting strategy, a tactic which was not a prerequisite for testing for the rank of sergeant.

In early 2005, I enrolled in graduate school for the spring semester, taking course work in human resources, and a few months later, Hubert was promoted to lieutenant. Soon thereafter, with nearly forty years on the job, Hubert announced his retirement. He retired as a legend who will be inducted into the Myrtle Beach Police Hall of Fame with such officers as Henry Howard Scarborough, Lieutenant P. I. Brown, Captain V. W. Strickland, and Patrolman First Class Joseph J. McGarry. The hall of fame was a place created in the minds of aspiring Myrtle Beach police officers, a place where officers dreamed their names would eventually be etched.

Hubert's retirement left me working alone out of a cubicle that was "coincidently" and conveniently located right beside the workspace for the Internal Affairs Office of Professional Standards. With Hubert no longer there to deflect arrows being shot in my direction, I tried to tiptoe lightly and avoid any unforeseen land mines. The warrant stats that I was required to submit each month repeatedly showed positive strides being made in the amount of arrests involving active warrants. This caught the critical eye of Chief Small, and even though I had already completed my six-month prison sentence, with no time credited for good behavior, the chief left me working on outstanding warrants.

The irrefutable facts were that once specific attention was given to these outstanding warrants, fugitives were being apprehended, which expedited criminal cases through the judicial system, strengthened police relations with victims of crimes, and assisted in maintaining security for our residents and visitors to the area by getting wanted criminals off the streets. As a result, Chief Small appointed me as a liaison for the police department with the United States Marshal Service, and I was sworn in as a special deputy with the marshals in December 2005. In April, 2006, I sent a memorandum to express my intent to compete in the sergeant promotional process:

To: Chief Wade Small
        Captain Fran Gilford
From: Investigator Brenda Christy
Subject: Police Sergeant Promotional Process
Date: 4/9/2006

Please accept this letter as my request to compete in the 2006 Sergeant Promotional Process. I have been employed with the police department since November 1987 and served as police investigator from October 1999 until present. I am a March 2006 graduate of Webster University with a master of arts in human resource development.

I have not had any preventable accidents, written reprimands, or suspensions from duty in the year prior to this announcement date. I have participated in campaigns for the United Way, American Heart Association, Grand Strand Leadership food drive, Christmas exchange gift tree for the Horry County Shelter home, Red Cross Heroes campaign, and the Horry County Disabilities and Special Needs fundraiser. I also am currently involved in the Police Unity Tour to raise monies for the National Law Enforcement Officers Memorial and the C.O.P.S. (Concerns of Police Survivors).

From my involvement with the Police Unity Tour, I have begun to organize a project designed to raise money for the family of Henry Howard Scarborough, the first Myrtle Beach police officer killed in the line of duty in 1949. These funds would help compensate Officer Scarborough's last living relative, his daughter, Doris Scarborough-Owens.

After completing a written project and an oral interview, the scores were calculated, and I learned I ranked number two, behind the top scorer, Investigator Jesse Bermudez, after Chief Small sent out a memorandum listing the official rankings:

**City of Myrtle Beach Police Department
Interoffice Memorandum**

To: All Department Personnel
From: Chief Wade S. Small
Subject: Results of the 2006 Sergeant's Promotional Exam/Process
Date: 05-15-06

First off, I'd like to congratulate the five candidates who competed in the 2006 sergeant's exam. I was extremely happy w/the quality of performances by all of the candidates. It's very evident that all of the candidates took this challenge seriously, and I commend them all for their efforts.

The results of the promotional process will create a promotional pool for any vacancies in the rank of sergeant for the remainder of 2006, and up until April 22, 2007.

At the present moment there is not an available slot for the position of police sergeant. The following ranking is a result of the recently completed process and will be used to aid in my selection of the next sergeant if and when a vacancy exists, and thereafter any additional slots that surface.

1. Inv. Jesse Bermudez
2. Inv. Brenda Christy
3. Inv. Ed D'Antonio
4. Inv. Timmy Alexander
5. Pfc. Rob Bedell

Each respective Division Commander will be available to discuss the strengths and weaknesses of each candidate in an effort to guide and counsel them towards their future goals as department supervisors. Good luck and I appreciate your hard work!

Cc: Post (Annex, LEC, Substation)

The year 2006 to 2007 was shaping up to be what appeared to be stellar year for me. In June 2006, I completed an application for Leadership Grand Strand, hoping to enhance my leadership skills to make me even more promotable. Leadership Grand Strand is an intense, nine-month program and is sponsored by the Myrtle Beach Chamber of Commerce. Criteria for selection include evidence of leadership abilities, potential to provide leadership to the Grand Strand, interest in community affairs, desire to expand volunteer involvement, and commitment to become more involved in the Grand Strand. Donna McFarland was an alumna of this program, and to my delight, she gave her endorsement for my commitment to go through this rigorous, time-consuming curriculum. On June 15, 2006, Donna McFarland sent a recommendation letter to the executive director for Leadership Grand Strand on my behalf. This endorsement letter would become an important legal document, as she would later give conflicting testimony concerning my leadership abilities in the city grievance proceedings and then again in her sworn affidavit prepared for the court.

In July 2006, the number-one ranked candidate, Jesse Bermudez, was promoted to sergeant. After receiving another "substantially exceeds expectations" rating on my yearly performance evaluation in August 2006 and a number of verbal and written accolades from the US Marshals Service, I was hopeful Chief Small would promote me to the rank of sergeant when the next position became available. I had graduated from Webster University with a master of arts degree in human resource development, was recognized as the Outstanding 2006 Graduate Student of the Year, and spoke at the graduation ceremonies. Innuendos of my forthcoming promotion to sergeant quickly ricocheted throughout the police department as I sat ready on the tarmac, eager to take flight.

7

THE BEEHIVE

In November 2006, Chief Small moved me into the Street Crimes Unit as a unit supervisor, specifically in charge of "B"-bracket officers. The lateral transfer gave me additional manpower for warrant service, but it also shouldered me with a multitude of additional assignments when not working joint operations with the US Marshals Service. I was skeptical of Chief Small's motive for prompting my transfer into the Street Crimes Unit, a unit being overseen by Lieutenant Donna McFarland.

The move was improper and put me in an awkward position after Lieutenant McFarland redacted her account of the sexual harassment incident. My wounds hadn't completely scabbed over yet, and unluckily, Lieutenant McFarland would now be in control of the denial for my specialized training requests, as well as be able to voice her disapproval for my suitability for promotion to sergeant, while putting her prejudicial pen marks on my employee performance evaluation.

Also, figuring into this intricate mathematical equation was my newly appointed supervisor, Sergeant Ashley Prior. Ashley was an eager young woman, eleven years my junior, who was on the fast track within the department. She had the likeness of the fictional character Clarice Starling, a gifted FBI trainee in the movie *Silence of the Lambs*, played by actress Jodie Foster. With little or no supervisory experience, Ashley rapidly rose through the ranks at lightning speed, from police officer to corporal to investigator and on to sergeant, all while breaking the sound barrier at each brief stop. Ashley was perceived to be inexorable, and it was well known that she had her sights on making lieutenant.

Observations of Ashley revealed her inability to disguise her craving to have it all—career, marriage, children—and in my opinion, her need for attainment would cause her to sacrifice her soul, like Donna McFarland and many others. Yet, I respected Ashley and had a lot of admiration for her before I became one of her subordinates.

Upon taking my position as a supervisor in the Street Crimes Unit, I immediately took note of the preexisting friendships between Ashley and her subordinates. One of the subordinates candidly talked about going to Ashley's house to babysit her daughter while she and her husband went out to celebrate Valentine's Day; another bragged about going to Ashley's house to play video games with her husband. When playing devil's advocate for Ashley's fraternizing, I expressed my philosophy as their supervisor, "My office door is always open, but the door to my home is not."

The Street Crimes Unit was like a beehive; Ashley was the queen bee, and the worker bees swarmed around her with loyalty and submission. For their loyalty to her agenda, she authored radiant employee evaluations, with words flavored in honey for substandard performances, as well as bestowing a multitude of fringe benefits to them. Ashley theorized that keeping worker bees submissive and happy would catapult her into the next promotional ceremony, where Chief Small would proudly pin gold lieutenant's bars on her uniform collar.

Because of Ashley's own paranoia, she would inundate me with patronizing emails and spray me with questionable corrective action to create evidence that reflected I was an incompetent supervisor. On one occasion, I received disciplinary action for failing to handcuff a subject I arrested for assault. I had arrested a male and a female during a road-rage incident. When I was hired, the department issued me only one pair of handcuffs, which I had used on the large, agitated male. I then interviewed the other driver, a petite female who had been struck in the face by the male. She admitted to striking the male, and I placed her under arrest. I had no other handcuffs, but she was cooperative, had no weapons or contraband, and posed no threat to me. I determined that it was more beneficial to transport her to jail than wait for another officer to bring another set of handcuffs. Even though I articulated my reasoning to Ashley and the department had no formal procedure for handcuffing more than one arrestee at a time, Ashley proceeded with the documented counseling. This was one of many welts from "bee stings" I would receive throughout my duration as a supervisor in the Street Crimes Unit. Ironically, soon after I received this corrective action, the department began issuing each officer two pairs of handcuffs as part of the standard duty equipment.

Once I took on an active role as a street crimes supervisor and had daily interaction with the worker bees, Ashley would run interference by meeting regularly with my shift personnel behind my back. She took these opportunities to keep them unified with her while promoting to them that I was as noxious to the beehive as an exterminator with an endless supply of poisonous chemicals. Ashley reassured them that she was still the queen bee and encouraged them to sidestep me for their special requests and confer with her anytime I gave them assignments.

In January 2007, a promotional opportunity became available for the sergeant candidates from the existing promotional pool. I was next in line and patiently waiting to receive my assignment as the next shift sergeant, but the devastating news came when I read an email distributed to all police personnel that Chief Small had promoted the number-three candidate, Ed D'Antonio, to sergeant. I was appalled to receive this information by email and not to have received any consoling words from the chief or an explanation for the rationale behind his decision. It was hurtful that Chief Small authored and also authorized contentious corrective action that resulted in my removal from two prior promotional pools in which I was in line for promotion; however, having a solid existence in this pool and being the next in line allowed me to see light at the end of the tunnel. Instead, Chief Small hopscotched over my name to choose a candidate who ranked lower on the list, causing that light to flicker and fade.

The chief's repeated refusal to promote me was unrestrained discrimination, which became one basis of my lawsuit. After the lawsuit was filed, I obtained through the motion-of-discovery process, the handwritten interview notes from members of the sergeant's oral interview board. One of the panel members wrote that during Ed's interview, he disclosed to them, "I don't have formal supervisory experience...I have not been in a patrol car in seven years." The ranking order in the promotional pool became insignificant, and selecting Ed for promotion became more comparable to drawing straws, which appeared fairer than actually testing for the position.

Despite not being promoted, I continued supervising the Street Crimes Unit, unaware that the train was about to derail when I was obligated as a supervisor to address policy violations and other employee infractions as they came to light. One employee failed to attend mandatory racial-sensitivity training and adjusted her schedule without authorization from me to work an off-duty employment detail. On a separate occasion, the employee forged her time sheet to reflect that she was on duty, when in fact she was not working. Two other employees responded to a drug complaint and seized marijuana from a male suspect at his residence but did not arrest the drug user or even issue a courtesy citation for the drug violation. Then the officers failed to correctly log the marijuana on official police evidence and inventory paperwork.

I was oblivious to Ashley's panic that I would inhibit her progression up the career ladder and sabotage her promotional track record because my supervision had inadvertently sur-faced erroneous work within the unit. Knowing Lieutenant Donna McFarland's acquiescent character, Ashley launched a plan of attack by going to her and informing her that my management style was creating conflict and officers under my command wanted transfers.

My supervision of the unit became nothing more than me in a fishbowl. With hair raised on her back, Ashley was con-stantly peering into the bowl. Whenever I made supervisory decisions, she would drop her paw into the water and with claws extended, chase me around the fishbowl relentlessly. Ashley intentionally avoided one-to-one communication with me and instead used our email correspondences as a deliberate attempt to show me as an incompetent supervi-sor. There was, however, a time when Ashley came into my office, and at some point during her visit, our mothers both dying from cancer was mentioned. It became a lengthy con-versation. It was touching for me to hear Ashley reflect on the momentous influence her mother had on her life and her expression of the love between a mother and daughter. I, too, reflected fondly on my mother, whom I had been named after. Sadly, my mother's life had been cut short when she lost her battle with pancreatic cancer at the age of fifty-nine.

Shockingly, Ashley would later declare this conversa-tion had actually been a planned counseling session, where she addressed with me all my supervisory deficiencies. It became hard for me to see the glass as half full because of Ashley's underhanded conduct and Donna's "ready, fire, and then aim" approach to supervision. Working for Ashley and Donna became comparable to sampling chocolate from

Forrest Gump's candy box: "You never know what you're gonna get." Ashley continued her sales pitch to Donna that they needed to eliminate me from the Street Crimes Unit, and she took the bait, hook, line, and sinker.

8

A THORN IN MY SIDE

n February 2007, Ashley's perseverance paid off, and Chief Small ordered Lieutenant Kurt Heiden to conduct an investigation into my supervision of officers in the Street Crimes Unit. Notebooks and pens came out, and unlike in the cover-up of the sexual harassment investigation, tape-recorders were added for truthfulness. As the investigation began, the theme was the same: I was to blame for the train wreck.

During my taped interview, I complained about being pigeonholed and about being under such tremendous scrutiny. I said to Heiden, "People have complained on other supervisors every single day, and it doesn't amount to this—it's the stigma attached to this name, and I'm telling ya, I can't work like this anymore."

Heiden told me, "Brenda, everything that I have addressed with you or asked of you, you've been able to come back in detail, you know, with a good explanation of what you did

and all that, and that's what I was going to send to the chief."
Heiden informed me of some of the questions he asked my
subordinates: "Did she disrespect you, yell at you, fuss at
you?" I listened to the taped statements of my subordinates,
and the unanimous answer was "No."

I said to Heiden, "I didn't walk in here feeling like I had
done anything wrong; it's just the stress of going through
this."

During my taped interview, I made more than one request
for a meeting with Chief Small to inquire why I was being
treated differently than other supervisors. Chief Small immediately took up a boxing stance, refusing to meet with me and
then delivering three uppercut ultimatums to me: 1) ask for
a demotion and he would grant the request to remove me as
a supervisor, 2) voluntarily terminate my employment, or 3)
supervise however he deemed appropriate. My conclusion
was Chief Small hated me, and I contemplated how much
longer I could withstand working for a boss ruling over me
with an iron fist, who expressed his feelings of abhorrence
so blatantly to me.

On March 1, 2007, after the chief had refused to meet
with me, I contacted the city manager's office to request a
meeting with City Manager Todd Long. On March 2, 2007, I
received confirmation Long would meet with me and that
he had ordered Chief Small to open his office door to me as
well. The meeting with Chief Small was prearranged for the
morning of March 5, and a meeting with Long would follow
in the afternoon.

With anxiety building days before the meetings, I was
arbitrarily flipping through television channels when I

came upon a program with Dr. Charles Stanley of In Touch Ministries. In his preaching, he said in times of trial, "Fight your battles on your knees." I related his words to scripture, *Devote yourselves to prayer with an alert mind and a thankful heart.* **(Colossians 4:2, NLT)** Dr. Stanley's sermon was one of a series of promptings that I would receive over an extended period of time echoing the message for me to turn my life over to Christ. Some of my nonbelieving acquaintances told me that they were "too far gone for God's grace," and then exclaimed, "So why change now?" With certainty, I disagreed with their declaration. So before the meetings, I made sure I called upon my prayer warriors, requesting prayer for my situation. I also took Dr. Stanley's counsel and repeatedly got on my knees in prayer.

The morning of the meeting as I breached the door frame leading into Chief Small's office, I felt it was an experience reminiscent of being summoned to the principal's office. I was met with a disgusted look as Chief Small sat behind his mahogany desk in his high-back leather chair. Small tried to mask his irritation with me when he informed me that he wasn't concerned that I was meeting with his boss, the city manager, later in the day. But the steaming volcano erupted when Small could no longer hide his aggravation as he looked me in the eyes and called me "a thorn in his side." I knew at that point I would not be permitted to openly express my concerns and question Small for his discrimination and retaliation toward me, but with uncontainable tears streaming down my face, I held up my hand and begged Small not to "let his anger control his words for me." Chief Small's words that I was "a thorn in his side" were hurtful and pierced my inner being, while outwardly the stigma of his words latched onto my name.

After my plea for Small to consider his callous words toward me, he gained his composure and strapped on a poker face while advising me of his displeasure regarding the officers who had not made the proper drug arrest after seizing marijuana. Small shared his opinion that the Street Crimes officers had a propensity to go off on tangents. After previously reading Heiden's report and listening to the tape-recorded interviews, Small cleared me of any wrongdoing.

Chief Small concluded the meeting by announcing that I was to assume my supervisory duties in the Street Crimes Unit at which time he would give any of my subordinates a "free pass" to transfer out of the unit if they were disgruntled. Upon leaving the meeting, Donna McFarland stopped me in the police department parking lot and asked me if I was still going to meet with the city manager since the outcome of the internal investigation was presumably in my favor. I gave her an affirming nod as I swiftly walked to my police car, silently knowing of my full intention to inform the city manager of Small's deliberate discrimination and retaliation against me.

Later the same day, I sat down in the city manager's office at City Hall. I observed Long's framed law degree hanging on the wall behind his desk. I recalled that he had actually been the assistant city manager and assistant city attorney in 1985 and was appointed to city manager in 1986 by the council a year prior to me being hired. His tenure and law degree would indubitably give him an advantage in knowing certain parts of our conversation could be considered by the court as "protected activity," as he appeared cautious. This would be an exceedingly important point as the content of our lengthy conversation would be vastly arguable at a later time.

After we exchanged pleasantries, I opened up my menu, spooning out a buffet of issues to him, and by the end of the two-and-a-half-hour meeting, the city manager's plate was full. I gave him plenty to chew on when, without hesitation, I tearfully apprised him of the sexual harassment incident and the spurious investigation resulting in my two-day suspension and written reprimand, the taped-up photograph, and the chief's discrimination toward me by failing to promote me and not properly notifying me of his decision to promote a candidate who ranked lower in the promotional process. My irrepressible tears caused the city manager to confiscate a box of Kleenex for me as he appeared concerned with what I had told him and sensitive to the affects these incidents had on me.

However, Long's demeanor during our meeting would prove to be a charade when he was later served with a deposition subpoena for my lawsuit and his haughty personality was blatantly displayed during his testimony. I expressed my concern to the city manager over the internal investigation I recently endured, which was inconsistent with the treatment of other supervisors, and Chief Small's retaliation toward me with the severity of corrective action he had issued upon me. I made the city manager aware that I was uncomfortable with Donna McFarland being my superior because of the outcome of the sexual harassment incident, and I was fearful of further retaliation from Chief Small.

It was apparent the city manager needed some Tums for his noticeable indigestion, as he had a hard time swallowing the discrimination and retaliation by a department head whom he had appointed, but I offered a solution to Lieutenant McFarland and Chief Small having total control of my destiny when I presented the city manager with statistics and pie charts for the number of actively pending arrest warrants and the number of warrants that had been served after this assignment was given to me. I proposed that I be transferred into the clerk of court's office to work warrants as a full-time position while still holding my police authority and police retirement; I would be accountable to Chief Municipal Judge Janice Walter. As I left the city manager's office, I was hopeful for relief soon. I had no reason to feel differently.

With the investigation into the train wreck officially over, Donna was left still scratching her head, so she felt the need to illustrate blame by using a percentage formula. She advised that Heiden, after conducting his investigation, had declared that I was 30 percent at fault, and the officers were 70 percent at fault. I had never heard of this fuzzy math calculation until well after the investigation; even so, I resumed my supervisory responsibilities and none of my subordinates transferred out of the Street Crimes Unit while I was their supervisor.

Ashley continued to have no direct interaction with me through the month of March 2007, unless a chance encounter would occur while we were passing in the hallway. Ashley also continued to flood my email inbox as her main form of supervising me despite my intentional stops at her office to be cordial. On one occasion, I went to Ashley's office to advise her of a necessary foot surgery I needed to correct problems that had developed from an off-duty car wreck years earlier. While I was midsentence and before I could request time off from work, Ashley got up and left for a lunch appointment. Disappointed in her inattentiveness while I was addressing a medical issue, I went back out to oversee my shift still hopeful of soon receiving a resolution from the city manager.

But two years would pass, and after the city manager failed to act upon or stop the inequity or vengeance being directed toward me by Chief Small, my complaints of discrimination and retaliation snowballed into a lawsuit. The words Chief Small used to describe me then quickly grew legs and became a catalyst for "a thorn in my side" as a phrase that would be used in many of the legal arguments to further support Small's perceptible discrimination and retaliation toward me. Repeatedly hearing these words being thrown around and then rereading this language in all the legal documents continued to distress me. Once the city was officially served with my lawsuit, Chief Small tried to distance himself from his choice of vocabulary by adding words to his original statement to imply a different meaning. Regardless of Small's semantics, during Donna McFarland's sworn deposition testimony, she was asked if she explicitly heard Chief Small call me "a thorn in his side," and if I told her Chief Small's words hurt me.

Q: Were you in a meeting with Ms. Christy and the chief where he called her "a thorn in his side"?
A: Yes.
Q: And did she [Brenda] bring that up to you afterward?

A: Yes.

Q: And you mentioned that in here that that had hurt her [Brenda] deeply?

A: Un-huh [affirmative response]. Yes, I did. She did say that.

Q: And you heard him say that?

A: Yes.

After Donna's confirmation of what Chief Small had called me, Small's attempts to rephrase his words became nothing more than a deceitful translation for his Freudian slip.

In **(2 Corinthians 12:7–10 NIV)**, the apostle Paul told of a thorn in his flesh and how he asked God to remove it. When God denied Paul's request, Paul later became joyful to have the thorn in his flesh after realizing that God was with him and that was all he needed.

To keep me from becoming conceited because of these surpassingly great revelations, there was given me a thorn in my flesh, a messenger of Satan, to torment me. Three times I pleaded with the Lord to take it away from me. But he said to me, "My grace is sufficient for you, for my power is made perfect in weakness." Therefore I will boast all the more gladly about my weaknesses, so that Christ's power may rest on me. That is why, for Christ's sake, I delight in weaknesses, in insults, in hardships, in persecutions, in difficulties. For when I am weak, then I am strong.

I was constantly trying to unfasten Small's words from my name. It was like peeling layers from an onion. I always found myself blinking back tears the closer I got to the center of the onion. I incessantly attempted to diminish Small's description of me as just hollow words, but regardless of how hard I tried, I was unable to emulate the apostle Paul's content spirit for the thorn in his flesh in comparison to what was happening to me.

9

THE SCHOOL SHOOTING

riday, March 30, 2007, would not be an ordinary day at work for me, as my officers and I responded to a call of a school shooting at Myrtle Beach High School. Upon arrival at the school, I found the scene chaotic with hysterical parents fearing the high school had become the next Columbine; they began driving through police roadblocks to gain access to the school grounds. Trailing on the car bumpers of the out-of-control parents was every journalist imaginable from print and broadcast media, all descending on the school to record the events as they unfolded.

The majority of the police department's command staff arrived on scene and immediately called for detectives and crime-scene specialists to respond. I positioned some of my officers in areas around the school to protect the crime scene and assist evacuating students out of the building. I instructed my other officers to respond to the hospital to check on the victim and his injuries. Several hours later, we learned that there was not an active shooter inside the school, but a student had brought a loaded gun in his book bag and the gun accidentally discharged into his leg when he attempted to sit at his desk. I was relieved to learn the student's self-inflicted gunshot wound was not life threatening and that my officers and I were trained to handle an incident of this magnitude.

That afternoon, I was called into the conference room of the police department after another promotional opportunity became available. In the concise meeting, I learned from Captain Veit, Lieutenant McFarland, and Sergeant Prior that Chief Small had, once again, scrolled down the promotional list, this time to pick the candidate ranking last in the promotional pool, Rob Bedell.

The police department had a promotional process policy that established criteria for officers to advance through the chain of command. The policy stated that an individual must proceed through the ranks of corporal and investigator before he or she could advance to the rank of sergeant. I challenged Rob's eligibility based on this policy, which went into effect on January 1, 2001, and remained in effect as we competed in this promotional process in 2006.

During Rob's policing career with the Myrtle Beach Police Department, he was never promoted to the rank of corporal, which meant he did not meet the minimum qualifications to hold the rank of investigator or sergeant pursuant to city and departmental policy. Yet Rob, the number-five-ranked candidate in the promotional pool, a younger male with only a high-school education and no supervisory experience was selected for promotion over me. Small gave no explanation for his amendment of the current city policy, only offering that Captain Fran Gilford confirmed the eligibility of each candidate, so Rob remained a sergeant while eyebrows were raised over the obvious policy blunder.

By this time, the voice of reason in my head and the feeling of devotion to the police department within my heart were clashing with each other as I contemplated a consultation meeting with an attorney specializing in employment law. My objective was not to begin litigation proceedings against the city but to find the path of least resistance to ending the discrimination and retaliation against me and from that point, move forward. I was organically naive, walking blindly into this process, as I had never before consulted an attorney for a personal matter.

I was a veteran of criminal law and courtroom testimony, but I would soon learn that civil litigation was a breed of its own. In the middle of trying to make this nail-biting decision and three days after the school shooting, Sergeant Ashley Prior received an email accolade from a crime-scene specialist after he first spoke with Lieutenant McFarland about my supervision during the chaotic incident.

From: Vick Dionne
Sent: Tuesday, April 03, 2007 9:36AM
To: Ashley Prior
Cc: Brenda Christy
Subject: School Shooting

On 03-30-07, I was on call when the school shooting occurred. I heard Pfc. Clark on the radio and thought he did well getting the info out under the circumstances. I then heard the radio turn into a quagmire of people talking over each other until some order was brought to this incident many minutes later. The one person that stood out was Inv. Christy. I had never worked for or with her so I didn't know what she was capable of in a crisis, but when she keyed up on the radio she didn't waste time with unnecessary radio chatter. Unlike many of the people that day her communications were to the point and very well stated.

The first people arriving were attempting to do many things such as secure the school from people going in and out and make sure the inside threat was ended. It took a large number of personnel to control the school's access points and was taxing on the patrol shift. Two officers were sent to an access point but they were being pulled from the road. Inv. Christy directed them to stay on the road and her officers would handle this access point. This action alone wasn't what grabbed my attention. It was the way she conducted herself on the radio. Amidst all the chaos and people talking over each other she was able to stay calm, transmit her commands, and have everyone receive them in a manner that was easily understood and to the point without leaving any question as to what was said. She then simply allowed everyone else to continue with the incident.

The next time I heard Inv. Christy on the air was when someone on scene asked for an officer that was still on the road to go and secure the suspect at the hospital. Once again Inv. Christy took charge, instructed that officer to stay on the road and her people would handle the hospital. The second time I heard Inv. Christy on the radio was no different than the first. Her instructions were once again easily understood and to the point without leaving any question as to what was said. This was the last time I heard Inv. Christy on the radio.

I spoke with Lt. McFarland about what I had observed that day and she said I should get up with you since you were her immediate supervisor. I must say there are those we all remember on the radio because they never stop talking but Inv. Christy was the one who grabbed my attention this time. It was not that she spoke a lot but instead it was what was spoken and how it was put over the air.

With this accolade and the internal investigation behind me, the dust had settled, so I put my list of attorneys in my back pocket and attempted to handle workplace matters on my own. Unfortunately, a dust bowl would form when I expressed my concerns to Lieutenant Donna McFarland about how Sergeant Ashley Prior was continuing to supervise me with emails. A day later, on April 18, 2007, I was called into a meeting with Donna McFarland and Ashley Prior. The meeting began with Ashley barking at me, "I'm not happy with you!" She continued by telling me that I was being disciplined for going over her head to complain to Donna about her. This idle threat of discipline was ludicrous—nothing more than Ashley's paranoia bleeding through her fury. I knew if the concern with an immediate supervisor was intolerable, going to the next overseeing supervisor for assistance and a resolution was acceptable protocol.

Donna sat idly behind her desk while the meeting turned into a shouting match between Ashley and me. The high-velocity volleys continued being served back and forth while Donna's head moved from left to right as she waited to see which one of us was going to score match point. As the match headed into extra sets, the needle on Donna's intervention meter remained stuck on zero. After several fouls, the verbal tennis match ended when an office assistant interrupted to make sure no one had gotten struck with a tennis racket camouflaged as office furniture.

Days later, I checked my personnel file and discovered that Ashley's threatened discipline for "going over her head" was not in the file and—of no surprise to me—there was no documented corrective action for the mutual verbal combat between Ashley and me in Donna's office. I knew from my supervisory experience that if I received discipline for insubordination, Ashley would also have to receive some type of corrective action for her lambast on me, and a written reprimand in Ashley's personnel file would automatically eliminate her from the lieutenant promotional pool.

Even with no documented corrective action on file, I would still have reason for alarm, when Donna advised me that Ashley no longer wanted to be my immediate supervisor now that I had criticized her management style. Nine days after the confrontational meeting between Ashley and me, her wish was granted. I was removed as a supervisor, and my status as a liaison for the US Marshals Service was taken. Donna advised me that the removal of my supervisory responsibilities was a temporary decision and that I would maintain my rank as investigator.

As I continued to work in the Street Crimes Unit, it was hard to accept that I had been removed as a supervisor, knowing the real cause was Ashley's antagonism. However, I could have easily been transferred back into the Investigative Division and held the same rank of investigator because personnel working as detectives in that division did not have subordinates assigned to them. In fact, the primary responsibility of these ranking officers was managing their time and their assigned case files. They did not complete employee performance evaluations, sign off time sheets, or approve vacation requests, because they were not actively supervising anyone. I was certainly capable of doing the work of a detective; as Sergeant Tony Cherni, previous supervisor of the Investigative Division noted on my employee evaluation, while I was assigned to the investigative division, my case-file workload was the fifth highest within the unit.

Transferring me back into the Investigative Division was a fitting solution to keep Ashley content since she was obviously not going to be transferred or disciplined. However, moving me into this division would guarantee me the benefits of a take-home car and a clothing allowance, remuneration Chief Small had no intention of giving to me. I was about to venture into unknown territory, and I knew that I needed God's guidance and wisdom even though, at the time, I was still not allowing God to live through me.

When attempting to find a consultation appointment with an attorney, I was advised that I also needed to file a complaint with the South Carolina Human Affairs Commission

(SCHAC), which was the first mandatory step in reporting workplace misconduct. I knew nothing of this state agency or their purpose; however, upon visiting their website, I learned the South Carolina Human Affairs Law was enacted in 1972, creating SCHAC. One of the commission's primary functions was to investigate and attempt to resolve charges alleging unlawful discrimination based on race, color, national origin, religion, sex, age, and disability, and their jurisdiction covered both public and private sectors.

My own conclusions were SCHAC was big brother's watchful eye for safeguarding all South Carolina employees from unfair treatment and their activities were overseen by the governor's office. I called and spoke with Sarah Laxton, a SCHAC investigator with the intake referral division, to begin the process of filling out the required thirteen pages of forms and questionnaires not including several pages of amendments for my particular complaint. This would be the beginning of a remarkably long and arduous voyage with this state-run agency.

Throughout the remainder of April and into the beginning of May, my work schedule was day shift, still in the Street Crimes Unit but temporarily not supervising, by order of the chief. Rolling in with the month of May was the roaring sound of motorcycles as the city prepared for the annual spring Harley Davidson motorcycle rally. The police department took an all-hands-on-deck approach to this event; operational plans took form, and days off were cancelled for all officers. As the motorcycle rally got underway, Donna assigned me to work a twelve-hour night shift detail for the entire weekend under the supervision of the ill-famed Corporal Max Malone.

Switching me from day-shift to a night-shift schedule was not uncharacteristic for Donna McFarland considering her authority over me, but to violate the chain of command by having me report to and take orders from a lower-ranking male officer was inappropriate and peculiar. My assignment was posted on a duty roster for all my colleagues to view, and I was the only person assigned to report to a lower-ranking officer. I was well aware of Max's mortifying conduct of mercilessly verbally ridiculing officers in public and peppering their personnel files with nitpicking corrective action. I was uncomfortable with the assignment, but I worked the weekend detail before going to Donna to express my embarrassment and humiliation. After I spoke with Donna, she sent an email up the chain of command forewarning Chief Small and his command staff of my complaint. Her email would start an adverse series of email exchanges that would lay the pipe to help seal my fate.

10

THE DEMOTION

I was the focus of the morning email exchanges, as Lieutenant Donna McFarland struck the keyboard first when describing her account of my embarrassment at being assigned to work for a male of a lower rank to Uniform Patrol Captain Jerry Veit. Veit wasted no time banging out his recommendation to continue the email succession to Chief Small and Captain Bob Franklin.

From: Donna McFarland
Sent: May 22, 2007 09:30AM
To: Jerry Veit
Subject: Christy

I spoke to her this morning about being embarrassed from being told what to do by a Corporal. I advised that she would be working warrants this weekend to prevent further embarrassment. I advised when the decision was made to put her in an area to work for Harley weekend that the Chief was fully aware of it. I said when we have special events the special events officer gives orders out for others to follow. She disagreed saying per regulation she should not take orders from a Corporal. I advised per regulation 101 Section 2, Chief Small could make a decision to do this. I told her not to further discuss personnel matters with outside agencies but to come to me if she has a problem. She said she didn't say anything derogatory and that the agent had asked about the diamond on her sleeve (that signified her rank). She said she didn't want anyone to get in trouble over this, but it really upset her. She said even yesterday after telling me, she went home and couldn't sleep because she was afraid that she would end up being the one in trouble, and it would come back on her, just as with me telling her not to discuss personnel issues with other agents. I advised Inv. Christy to type up an itinerary for me for Saturday and Sunday and work an 8-hour day 08:00–16:00.

From: Jerry Veit
Sent: May 22, 2007 09:45AM
To: Wade Small
CC: Bob Franklin
Subject: FW Christy

There is no winning with her. She will twist everything that is said and done to her way of thinking only. I feel more now than ever that she needs to be demoted or fired. The agent asking about the diamond is something most would ask about not meaning that there was an issue except what she must have brought up?

Lieutenant McFarland and Chief Small, as usual, were unsympathetic to the situation they had created for me and gained support from others in the command staff when it was concluded that I had made a much bigger deal of the matter than warranted. Without a formal investigation into my complaint and within fifteen minutes of the first email exchange, it was decided that I would be demoted or fired, and just as McFarland had expressed in her email to Jerry, that "I was concerned I would end up being the one in trouble," that was exactly what was going to happen just days after I had officially complained.

Once all the emails had been exchanged and read, I surmise, Chief Small had his finger on the trigger and was ready to fire when he realized that he didn't have the "smoking gun" he needed to finalize his vindictive plot against me. Small needed something to eclipse some of the most recent accolades in my favor. Chief Small then instructed Lieutenant McFarland to "create" documentation against me, and she enlisted the help of Sergeant Ashley Prior to put together what was later dubbed "the demotion notebook."

The "demotion notebook" contained solicited documentation from one captain, three lieutenants, and three sergeants; however, this created demotion notebook was never included in my personnel file or brought up in the grievance hearing. I only learned of the demotion notebook when it was submitted by the city's legal defense team during "first interrogatories and continuing request for production of documents and things through the motion-of-discovery process." During Donna McFarland's sworn testimony, in her deposition, she recalls the email exchanges and the creation of the "demotion notebook."

Q: Okay. She [Brenda] indicated to you that she was worried that she's going to get in trouble for complaining about this, is that correct?

A: Correct.

Q: When in fact she was going to be demoted?

A: Correct.

Q: Do you know what years she [Brenda] worked with Lieutenant Damons?

A: Not certain. I can guesstimate when she worked for Lieutenant Damons. I'm thinking maybe 1997...'98. Something like that maybe.

Q: So close to ten years before this is going on in 2007?

A: That's correct.

Q: So Bob Franklin is asking him...asking Lieutenant Damons to go back and generate reports on things that occurred ten years prior?

A: I think he said...and he said that Lieutenant Damons was going to create a report documenting some of the issues. That's what he said.

Q: Did you ever see the report that Lieutenant Damons prepared?

A: Yes.

Q: And it's dated 5/22/07?

A: Yes.

Q: And it was...and the first line says, "Yesterday you asked that I put some thoughts in writing concerning my evaluation of then Corporal Christy's performance as a first-line supervisor during the time that she was assigned as the section corporal for Narcotics and Vice years ago and if that opinion has changed at all since then and if so, why." So this report was created and had not been in her personnel file or had not been in existence until 5/22/07, is that correct?

A: That's what I understand, yes.

Q: All right. Now, do you have any idea why it would seem necessary that just a few days after she complained about being supervised by a male corporal, it would be necessary to go back and ask somebody to write a report about her performance from ten years prior?

A: I don't know…

Q: But you used that in—

A: …what their motive was.

Q: But you collected that information and included it—

A: For the notebook. I believe it was. That's why. If I remember, it was that gathering documentation that the chief requested for us to do, so I'm thinking that's why.

City policy requires that the city manager approve a demotion of an employee, so Chief Small used the created demotion notebook as his magic bullet to advise the city manager of his intention for the relegation. Without providing any feedback to the formal complaint I made to him weeks before, the city manager gave Chief Small the green light he needed to proceed with my demotion.

On the morning of May 28, 2007, I was once again called into the principal's office for another dreadful meeting with Chief Small. Looking for tripwire, I took short, hesitant steps into Chief Small's office. My reluctance to receive another tongue-lashing caused me to feel as though I was walking barefoot on thumb tacks; my feet could hardly move across the carpet on his office floor. I didn't know what to expect because of the residual memories that existed from being in his office before, but my first clue was seeing Chief Small holding paperwork in his hand.

It was a demotion memorandum he had authored, which was dated just four days after I complained to Lieutenant McFarland about being supervised by a lower-ranking officer. When Small began reading the memorandum word for word in a monotonic voice, it was like having a bucket of ice water thrown in my face.

To: Inv. Brenda Christy, Uniform Division
From: Chief Wade S. Small
Subject: Notice of Personnel Action
Date: 05-25-07

Pursuant to Article I, Section 10 of the Employee Handbook you are hereby notified that effective Monday, 05-28-07 you are being reduced in rank to Patrol Officer First Class (Grade 21-Step 46).

Your chain of command officers have worked diligently to afford you ample opportunities to develop leadership and supervision skills commensurate with your position/ rank as Police Investigator. Your failure to progress to an acceptable level, and your continued resistance and contempt for command officers who are responsible for guiding you and supervising you in an effort to get you into a position to lead officers in this department has left me no option but to remove you from a position with supervisory responsibilities.

You have demonstrated an extraordinary level of competence in your role in the Street Crimes Unit handling warrants and fugitives; however you have not been able to gain the necessary skills or respect from your subordinates required to lead them as a supervisory officer.

You will remain assigned to the Street Crimes Unit as the warrants/fugitive officer.

Pursuant to Article II, Section 10 of the Employee Handbook, you are entitled to appeal this decision. If you have any questions regarding this procedure, please contact my office.

Small got up to make a copy of the memorandum to give to me as I sat quietly, feeling as though I had just gone through childbirth without an epidural. I was in terrible, poignant anguish. In my state of incredulity, I had to focus on scripture to sustain me: *And we know that God causes everything to work together for the good of those who love God and are called according to his purpose for them.* **(Romans 8:28, NLT)**

While waiting on Small to return, I hit the rewind button in my mind and listened to his words over and over, never describing any specific incident or marginal work performance that would validate a demotion. The memorandum was vague and incomplete because the demotion was without cause. It was unadulterated retaliation. Even though there had been other city employees who had received voluntary or involuntary demotions without a reduction to their current salary, Chief Small exercised his position of authority to have my salary reduced from $53,118 to $48,125, giving further confirmation of his retaliatory motives. As if I hadn't suffered enough, before leaving Chief Small's office, I was ordered to change out my badge and uniform to reflect the newly inaugurated rank and to clean out my office by the close of the business day.

It was only by God's grace that I survived working the rest of my shift, as I was aimlessly walking through the halls trying to find myself. After I had changed my uniform and begun the process of finding boxes to clean out my office, rumors of my demotion spread like wildfire, and detectives lined up outside my door, watching me pack up my belongings. Their silence and the somber expressions on their faces were indicative that they were in disbelief just as much as I was. As hard as I tried not to cry, I could not stop the downpour of tears running down my face flooding the front of the new uniform shirt that I was ordered to wear.

As difficult as the day was, I was grateful that I made it home that evening and had my significant other, Magda, to fall back on for support. Magda was a highly motivated, extremely disciplined attorney from Poland with a brilliant mind. Juggling the ideas of practicing law in the United States or returning to Poland to continue pursuing her career aspirations, she secured a job as a paid intern with a law firm in Surfside Beach, and our paths had crossed through our jobs. She fascinated me with her ability to plan out each phase of her life and fulfill far-reaching goals she had set for herself. But as I paused during my time of anguish, I took note of striking resemblances between the ambitious personalities of Ashley and Magda.

Making the rank of lieutenant became the center of Ashley's soul, whereas being a superior attorney became the focal point of Magda's soul, while she unconsciously isolated God from her plans. This fortuitous connection between Ashley and Magda left me contemplating an **ah-ha moment: While on our journey, we often live the life we have planned for ourselves instead of the life God has for us.**

Even so, Magda's abstract mind and forward thinking were uplifting as my career hung in the balance and I hopelessly struggled to understand what had just occurred and how to overcome my adversities. I had hit a wall. To me, my self-esteem resembled a piece of soggy toast being scraped off a saucer and tossed into a trash can. Magda and I were both aware that our relationship had biblical consequences, but we found ways to falsely interpret God's Word and justify our feelings for each other. Our relationship was the only stable thing in my life at the time, but specific occurrences would later cause me to conclude God speaks to us through His Word, and frequently He will speak to us through events in our lives and through other people. I would eventually be convicted by the Holy Spirit through one of my neighbors, causing me to examine the conflict in my life and confront my transgression head-on.

Elsa lived directly across the street from me and had been my neighbor for many years. Even though she didn't stand much taller than five feet, she was hard to overlook because of her drill-sergeant moral fiber. When Elsa felt convicted or led by the Holy Spirit to express her position, her piercing brown eyes often penetrated through me as she shouted her unfiltered message from her pretend bullhorn. Being from Columbia, South America, Elsa's good-natured intent was often misunderstood by many because of cultural differences and her need for immediate compliance.

Like shooing a fly from potato salad at a picnic, I frequently shrugged my shoulders and waved my hand in the air, causing Elsa eventually to do an about-face and march in seemingly perfect cadence back to her house until she could find scriptural grenades to reinforce her message. I was fond of Elsa and in awe of her love for Jesus, but at the time, I was as enthusiastic to hear her importunate declarations as I was to find bug splatter on the windshield of my freshly washed car.

11

THE ATTORNEY

It was apparent, now more than ever, I would have to speak to an attorney, but I had legitimate stereotypes about lawyers that influenced me when weighing options for choosing legal counsel. My perception for experienced lawyers was that they were all money-driven and only wanted to represent clients in class-action cases, where the potential to be awarded millions in damages was most appealing to them. Those inexperienced attorneys newly admitted into the South Carolina Bar Association, I presumed, would be ones to latch on to any case, regardless of merit, and fight relentlessly in an attempt to establish their name. Neither typecast was helping me to commit firmly to seeking legal advice, but, if I had to get an attorney, I wanted the kind of representation with Erin Brockovich qualities.

Years ago, I absentmindedly watched the *Erin Brockovich* motion picture based on a true story of a woman working as a file clerk in a law office who gained the trust of several residents living in Hinkley, California, with serious medical conditions. Brockovich became a victim's advocate and a crusader when she uncovered a hidden secret of an energy corporation knowingly contaminating the ground water with hexavalent chromium, which was to blame for the illnesses of the residents. The movie exemplified the real-life heroics of a person using the compassion and tenacity within her soul to unselfishly find justice for others. I was a cop, not an employment law specialist. I needed an attorney who would wrap his or her brain around what I had gone through, decipher the chief's pretext basis for not promoting me and the wrongful demotion, and apply these acts of discrimination and retaliation under laws, such as Title VII of the Civil Rights Act of 1964 and other specific applicable federal and state laws.

But if I could not find the likeness of Erin Brockovich in an attorney, the thought of ending up on the other side of the pendulum with a rabid lawyer to sic on the chief and city manager was of no consolation to me. I began pouring over lawyer referrals and studying all their credentials, their years as a practicing attorney, as well as the distinguishing titles that people liked to attach to their name.

While reviewing numerous attorney credentials, I became too focused on which attorneys had received the Super Lawyers of South Carolina and Best Lawyers in America honors and had the prestigious Matindale-Hubbell "AV" rating for quality and integrity. Truthfully, in this life, one's nationality, race, education, or social position is unimportant; such things aren't so significant. Whether a person has Christ is what really matters. For me, the true question for an attorney should have been, "Is he/she a Christian?" instead of how many titles, promotions, or accolades he or she had accumulated.

At the beginning of June 2007, I was in back-and-forth correspondence with the SCHAC intake investigator for my formal complaint and continuing to shorten the attorney consultation list. I was also still committed to exhausting all of the in-house administrative remedies in order to get resolution and handle the wrongful demotion at the lowest level possible. I sent Chief Small a memorandum dated June 6, 2007:

Chief of Police, Wade S. Small:

This letter is in appeal to the notice of personnel action given on May 28, 2007, pursuant to Article II, Section 10 of the Employee Handbook with reference to the reducing in rank to Patrol Officer First Class.

Over the last several days, I have analyzed details connected with my supervising in the Street Crimes Unit, as well as correspondence with previous subordinates, and Chain of Command, which left me unclear as to the severity of this corrective action. Article I, Section 10 of the Employee Handbook, defines several reasons for demotion; my assumption from the notice of personnel action is that my reduction in rank was the result of "marginal performance." A review of all disciplinary action in my personnel file from when I began supervising the Street Crimes Unit to May 2007 does not show any documentation to sustain marginal supervisory performance. Additionally, an assessment of my most recent annual employee performance evaluations confirms that my job performance substantially exceeds expectations.

An examination of the aforementioned did not illustrate a continued resistance and contempt for command officers or lack of respect from subordinates as described in the notice of personnel action given, May 28, 2007.

The inquiry February 27, 2007, involving my subordinates and then the meeting with you on March 5, 2007, concluded that I was supervising effectively. This leaves me under the assumption that the reduction in rank occurred as a result of some type of incident transpiring after March 5, 2007, until May 28, 2007, when the notice of personnel action was given.

With no forewarning orally or in writing from any of my command officers concerning contempt for their authority or any explicit illustrations of marginal supervisory performance while in the Street Crimes Unit, it is difficult to comprehend this dramatic disciplinary decision.

I respectfully request consideration to be reinstated to the rank of Police Investigator.

On June 8, 2007, before I was given the opportunity to contest the unjustified demotion through the grievance process and before I was able to have a chance to exhaust all administrative remedies, Chief Small promoted Corporal Matt Conrad to the rank of investigator to fill the opening created as a result of my demotion. Within the same week, I selected an employment law attorney with a thick résumé of qualifications and drove to the South Carolina Human Affairs Commission in Columbia to meet with the intake investigator to finalize my formal complaint with my public sector employer. When I arrived at the SCHAC building, I was escorted into the office area where there were desks within cubicles, and on each desk were stacks of files, but I saw no one sitting behind any of the desks actively working. My recollection of these cubicles, absent the workers in them, would later give clarification for the snail's pace my case would take on as it began being shuffled through this assembly line. After finalizing this paperwork, I drove to the other side of Columbia where I met with Attorney Martha Barnwell.

Martha glanced over the final draft of the SCHAC complaint, which I had filled out on my own. She gave no input to the correctness of the completed forms or any suggestions on intertwining the violations of law with the failure to promote and the ultimate demotion by my employer. Instead, Martha signed and notarized the forms and entrusted me to drive them back across town to their final resting place in a file on a desk at the SCHAC office. I thought this was standard protocol and any modification and application of law would be done between the representing attorney and the SCHAC case investigator; however, as the process proceeded, this would be one of a few significant gaffes that would be exposed after the city would leave me no other choice but to file a lawsuit against them.

After leaving Columbia, I drove straight through North Carolina and Virginia to spend Father's Day weekend with Dad in West Virginia and share details of my meeting with my newly retained attorney. Dad was a retired coal miner with three daughters and a son. Upon retiring, he opened up Christy Machine, a machine shop that built and restored mining locomotives. I bragged that Dad had a mind comparable to Albert Einstein's, as he was a self-taught genius who could build anything from just a mental picture.

Dad had worked hard his entire life, and for many years, his business struggled just to make payroll, but whether Dad was giving to a customer or to one of his children, stepchildren, or grandchildren, he always gave more than he had. It had always been difficult for Dad to show emotion or say, "I love you." He just wasn't programmed that way; I had never seen Dad cry, not even when he buried both of his parents or when I moved away from home. Over the years, I would sporadically converse with him over my belief in Jesus Christ. I always believed Dad was not an atheist but thought he displayed agnostic characteristics, as he always needed proof for those miracles recorded in the Bible that had no scientific justification.

As with so many of us, a perplexing question for him had always been, if God was such a loving God, then why did he allow tragedies to happen in the world we lived in? I hadn't attended any theology courses, so it was difficult to provide all the answers needed to convince Dad of the value placed on his soul, but I did know through scripture:

Now we see things imperfectly as in a poor mirror, but then we will see everything with perfect clarity. All that I know now is partial and incomplete, but then I will know everything completely, just as God knows me now. **(1 Corinthians 13:12, NLT)**

It would repeatedly annoy me when I would ask Dad to pray for me regarding my situation at work and he would always say, "I'll keep my fingers crossed." I became dedicated to pray with Sabina and her parents for my dad's soul and his salvation, but even with our spiritual differences, I experienced firsthand Dad's undeniable love for me when without hesitation, he promised that he would financially help me for the duration of this litigation. Prematurely, Dad and I were optimistic that now that I had legal representation, the city would agree with me and resolve the discrimination and retaliation quickly and amicably in my favor.

I returned to Myrtle Beach and sent a formal request to City Manager Todd Long on June 27, 2007, requesting to appeal my demotion to the grievance committee. The grievance committee was the next step in the administrative remedies process, but it was a procedure I knew little about. Considering my recent demotion, I postponed my necessary foot surgery to avoid any further retaliation for requesting medical leave. Since I no longer had my own office, I resumed my assigned workspace cubicle beside the Internal Affairs Office of Professional Standards. For me, going from having my own office to working out of a cubicle felt like going from a condominium to a dungeon, and the demotion caused many of the officers to ostracize me. In confidence, some officers told me that they feared retaliation from the command staff if they were observed openly communicating with me. It was painful to exist in near solitude, but eventually some of the ignominy and cynicism created by the demotion lost its foothold and officers would periodically break their silence while Chief Small and his entourage made the retaliation less noticeable.

12

THE GRIEVANCE

Be strong and courageous. Do not be afraid or terrified because of them, for the LORD your God goes with you; he will never leave you nor forsake you. **(Deuteronomy 31:6, NIV)**

was notified by Human Resource Director Calvin Rabin of the hearing guidelines that had been set forth for this type of procedure and later by Human Resource Administrator Carmen Rutenberg that the grievance committee members would reconvene on July 11, 2007, to hear my appeal. With less than two weeks to prepare, Magda and I rolled up our sleeves and worked on creating a time line of events within the year 2006 to 2007, leading up to my demotion, while using numerous accomplishments and accolades from over the years to piece together my work as a public servant for the City of Myrtle Beach.

Going into the grievance proceedings, Chief Small knew the grievance panel would be made up of almost all city department heads, handpicked by the city manager for a three-year appointment. Small was familiar with each of these individuals, having been in enough closed-door meetings with them. At the onset, all parties agreed that the meeting would be closed to the public with only scheduled witnesses admitted. I knew I was playing a high-stakes game, but unknown to me, the deck was already stacked and I had a better chance of winning at a card table on the Las Vegas strip than winning the vote of this panel to reinstate my rank.

The committee chairman, Pete Edgeworth, dealt me the first round of cards for this poker game and then made me show my hand while Chief Small clandestinely arranged his cards. I threw down what I thought was an ace when I grabbed the attention of the grievance committee members with a fifty-one-slide PowerPoint presentation. I produced pictures, statistics, and other documentation of a nearly twenty-year police career; I went into the exceptional year leading up to my demotion and highlighted the managing struggles in the Street Crimes Unit, the substandard work by the subordinates, and my hypothesis of the reason for my demotion.

When it was Chief Small's turn to throw his cards on the table, he held up my personnel file as his trump card. Small chose to magnify discipline that had absolutely nothing to do with his decision to demote me, and this made his trump card look more like a joker's wild card. Chief Small and I would continue to hurl rocks at each other for nearly five hours, with no one taking a break for lunch and neither one of us taking any recuperation time from rocks that landed direct hits.

Trying to keep his house of cards from falling and not to be outdone, Small pleaded with the committee members to bring in his backup arsenal, testimony from Lieutenant Donna McFarland followed by testimony from Sergeant Ashley Prior. The planned weaponry did not have me running for cover, but Donna and Ashley did do a good job promoting Chief Small's propaganda. Their lengthy testimonies were riddled with distortions and fabricated reasons for my demotion. After the last hand was dealt and the last rock was thrown, I packed up the PowerPoint projector and gave thanks to God for giving me the courage to face the chief and his peers. I also thanked God for the opportunity to bring to the forefront the real reasons behind my demotion and for being able to account for the contributions my career had made for the city.

I did not readdress all of the discrimination and retaliation with the grievance committee since I had already had a substantive meeting with the city manager and I was of the opinion that he would help me. I also presumed that the grievance committee did not have any more jurisdiction over my complaint than the city manager. I left hopeful that despite any hidden expectations from Chief Small, the committee members would guard their souls and make the correct decision to recommend my rank be reinstated to police investigator.

As optimistic as I was, on July 18, 2007, the grievance committee recommended to uphold the personnel action

Chief Small imposed upon me to include the salary reduction. City policy stipulated the city manager must review the committee's findings, and he had the authority to uphold, modify, or overrule the decision.

Because I named the city manager in my complaint to the SCHAC, he directed Assistant City Manager Regis Abrams to review the committee's findings. On July 25, 2007, I received a memorandum from Abrams advising that he concurred with the committee's findings and concluded the action taken by Chief Small was "complete and proper." This was disappointing news, but there would be more road-rash on my journey as my yearly employee evaluation was due within a few weeks.

After receiving the final ruling from the assistant city manager and weeks after I filed an official complaint with the State Human Affairs Commission, Ashley would author the lowest performance evaluation of my entire career, a one percent merit bonus. Signatures and reaffirming comments for this horrendous evaluation also came from Lieutenant McFarland, Captain Veit, Chief Small, and City Manager Long.

After I reviewed the city manager's comments on my evaluation and his signature endorsing this atrocious representation of my work, the reality that he was not as concerned with my dire situation as he pretended to be in our meeting and that he shirked his responsibility to probe into my complaints was all too apparent. I had reached the top of the city government totem pole with no relief. I believed I only had two options: 1) resign to avoid further retaliation, or 2) file a lawsuit.

This was an extremely difficult decision, which made it hard not to cover my head with a pillow and curl up in a fetal position, hoping it was all just a bad dream. Speed-dialing every Christian in my phone contacts, I called upon everyone to commit the matter to dedicated prayer. Shortly thereafter, a stirring within my soul guided me to continue my employment, while foreseeing my discrimination and retaliation complaint would sprout in the SCHAC system, inevitably budding into a lawsuit as the complaint became rooted.

13

PRIOR-GATE

n August 2007, while Ashley was busy making those final annotations on my yearly evaluation, her malicious supremacy over me would come to a momentary standstill when she would be confronted with her own workplace cataclysm. Officers scurried through the hallway chanting, "Rome is falling," when news that a select few in the police department's elite club were involved in an argument after two of the officers were found in a precarious position with adulterous connotations. An inquest would be unavoidable when the four officers—Ashley; her husband, an investigator with the police department; a female investigator; and her husband, a K-9 handler with the police department— brought their commotion into the police department, landing on Mahogany Row in front of the chief and his command staff, on the same afternoon as the episode had erupted.

Officers labeled the scandalous matter "Prior-Gate," the last names of two of the officers involved. Almost immediately, the inquiry took the same blind-eye approach as the 2002 sexual harassment investigation, primarily because of who was involved. Weighing the potential ramifications to these chosen few, the internal investigation would take on a likeness to the cover-up that occurred in the Penn State–Joe Paterno tragedy, but after allegations of criminal misconduct surfaced, involving an altercation and one of the officer's firearms, the chief would not be able to exercise his preferential treatment entirely because the investigation would be jointly conducted with the State Law Enforcement Division and the results later reviewed by the Fifteenth Judicial Circuit Solicitor's Office.

Through subpoena, the South Carolina Criminal Justice Academy divulged "Personnel Change in Status—Report of Separation Forms" that were filled out by Chief Small after the investigation reached its official conclusion. These forms were mandatory and had to be sent to the academy whenever an officer was no longer employed in a law-enforcement capacity. Of no surprise, instead of the plausible demotions or terminations, Chief Small allowed two of his golden children to resign while the other two retained their positions within the department. Ashley was still my direct supervisor, and I wasn't sure what changes, if any, this incident would have on my current working conditions. Ashley took a requested leave of absence, while scores of officers took pleasure in the humiliation this throbbing debacle caused for her and the others involved in "Prior-Gate."

While exhibiting their malevolent attitudes, officers proclaimed this was "karma" and offered me the opportunity to jump on their bandwagon. But because of everything I had already emotionally endured, pain and hurt had a firm grip on my soul, which gave me an authentic empathy for Ashley's emotional turmoil, no matter how much I loathed her treatment of me. I prayed for healing for Ashley and the others and that each would do some personal reflection for the sake of change.

After Ashley returned from her leave of absence, unfortunately, it was business as usual when she continued with her customary reign over me. Knowing what she had just been through, I was saddened by her unaffected demeanor, as I recalled the words from an American poet and critic Archibald MacLeish, who once said, "There is only one thing more painful than learning from experience, and that is not learning from experience." Throughout the course of our journey, at some point, everyone living on earth will suffer some form of adversity, and admittedly, I would have to keep reminding myself of MacLeish's words and Bible scripture as I walked through my own difficulties: *Because you know that the testing of your faith develops perseverance.* **(James 1:3, NIV)** Even though I wasn't directly involved in this lamentable occurrence, it was metaphoric of the day-to-day operations within the police department, considering that I had just been demoted two months prior for pretext reasons.

September 2007, my complaint with SCHAC was set up to go through the commission's voluntary mediation program during which time I signed a mediation participation agreement as well as the commission's statement of confidentiality. After I coordinated with my attorney and the city's human resource administrator, the mediation hearing was set for October 2, 2007, at the SCHAC building in Columbia, South Carolina.

At the beginning of the meeting, I met two of the city's three attorneys, Ted Ellmore and Kate Thiel, along with the SCHAC mediator, Ray Thorpe. After brief opening statements by my attorney and the city's legal counsel, followed by an account from me, we broke off into separate rooms. As Martha and I patiently waited for Ray to speak with us privately, I remembered telling Martha during one of our previous meetings that I felt like Chief Small hated me. Martha quickly advised me, "It's not against the law to hate someone." I thought to myself, *Well, it should be!* Ray Thorpe, in the role as mediator, finally joined us, and I was hopeful a resolution could be obtained; however, after five hours, we were at an impasse, and we concluded the meeting.

It had been a long and difficult day, so I stopped outside a church when leaving Columbia long enough to have a phone conversation and pray before making the seemingly endless drive back to Myrtle Beach. I returned to work the following day and waited to hear from my attorney or a representative from the SCHAC. On October 4, 2007, I received notification from the SCHAC apprising me that my complaint had been forwarded for investigation and assigned to Diane Fraser.

Days before Christmas 2007, the third member of the city's legal team, Attorney Caylee Shultz, provided a lengthy rebuttal to my complaint submitted to SCHAC. There were many misrepresentations of facts in the information she provided, and I would feel compelled to address some of these falsehoods at a later date. In part, the city contended in the rebuttal that my supervisory duties were removed

in April 2007 while the department considered my continued employment and that the grievance committee upheld
the demotion. Additionally, the city denied that I ever complained that I was a victim of discrimination or retaliation.

January 2008 left me to fend for myself at work with little
or no contact from Martha or Diane. If there was any correspondence, it was initiated by me to inquire about any investigative developments or the next step in the legal process.
As weeks turned into months, it became a "hurry up and
wait" exercise with my patience. I started to wonder if the
city fired me, if I would even be able to get a job in a pie fac-
tory, as my self-esteem continued to sink to lower levels than
I thought were possible. I needed to find a distraction to keep
from feeling sorry for myself. At work, regardless of where I
walked, I was always the elephant in the room, and it was an
awful aura. Knowing that God had blessed me with a giving
spirit within my soul, I wanted to find good in the world again,
so I embarked on a mission trip to Zambia, South Africa.

My trip overseas would not commence until the first day
of August, but for the next several months, I would divide my
time between surviving the booby traps at work and completing a mandatory list of requirements that must be met
prior to purchasing my airline ticket. Each missionary was
responsible for raising close to three thousand dollars, in
addition to obtaining a passport and numerous immuniza-
tion shots and passing a physical examination. My continued
prayer was for God to give me peace, joy, and purpose for
my life, long after my return from this third-world country.

February 2008 would be the start of my first fundraiser
for the mission trip. I registered for a sixty-four-mile bicycle

ride sponsored by Michelob Ultra, which occurred the day after the Myrtle Beach Marathon. I drafted a sponsor letter and solicited friends and coworkers for a donation for every mile I completed. I thanked God for the spectacular weather he delivered for the ride as I crossed the finish line, raising nearly $1,300 for the trip.

I would attend weekly meetings with the other missionaries to pray, share testimonies, and give inspirational updates on our fundraising progress. We were a diverse group of nineteen men and women, married, widowed, and single, ranging in age from twelve to seventy-five.

One of the most regrettable fundraising memories I had was during a golf tournament our mission team sponsored. Jill, one of the missionaries, coerced me into riding on a golf cart with her to check on the needs of the golfers. Once we were far enough from civilization, she ambushed me with a barrage of questions concerning my sexual orientation. I was embarrassed and horrified. As I sat silent while Jill drove us back to meet up with the other missionaries, a scripture came to mind:

> They said to him, "Teacher, this woman has been caught in the act of adultery. Now in the Law Moses commanded us to stone such women. So what do you say?" And as they continued to ask him, he stood up and said to them, "Let him who is without sin among you be the first to throw a stone at her." **(John 8: 4–5, 7, ESV)**

It was too late to turn back from the mission trip to Africa, but Jill's scheme had once again upset the apple cart with my internal struggle between scripture and the life I was living.

Trying to find a church that would see my indisputable love for God, despite my sexual orientation, was like fitting a square peg into a round hole. While actively dealing with the tribulations of my job, judgment from the church was the last thing I needed to undergo. Every time the question would rear its ugly head, my first instinct was to begin shopping to find a large enough church that Magda and I could attend without having crosshairs from the "holier-than-thou" group aimed on our backs.

In my own faith journey, I encountered many nonbelievers curious to know Christ but opting to forgo finding a personal relationship with their Savior because of bigotry and hypocrisy within the church. God would continue to speak to me through people, allowing specific individuals in my life for a reason and for a season. In hindsight, the length of the season was often dependent on me, and if I would respond to God's calling. There would be more pain and many more potholes in my road to redemption, but God's grace and unconditional love would eventually become amazingly clear to me during the course of my journey.

By July 2008, the status of my case with SCHAC had not changed and I wanted to get an update before leaving the country. I had heard nothing substantial since October 4, 2007, when my complaint had been forwarded and assigned to Diane Fraser. Despondent over the lack of headway made in my case, I went through then Governor Mark Sanford's office to get answers and make an inquiry on my behalf. I would later learn from then SCHAC Commissioner Jackson Wackerly Jr. that the agency was understaffed. Diane served as a division director in addition to her supervisory responsibilities. She also carried an investigative caseload of complaints for both employment discrimination and housing discrimination. Additionally, my complaint would be investigated on a first-come, first-served basis, at which time the commissioner gave no indication as to the number of complaints already filed ahead of mine. These factors would have an enormous impact on just how long I would wait for my complaint to be investigated, all while I continued to work for the city under Chief Small's authority.

14
AFRICA

pring and summer of 2008 were somewhat of a blur for me as the tourist season kept me busy at work. With the consequences of the housing market crash still forthcoming, there were signs that officer morale was also on the decline. Most officers were unable to fully predict the domino effect foreclosures and unemployment would have on tightening the belt on our police wages and benefits or that our nation's economy would slip into a recession. I didn't have time to analyze officer morale or the impact of our country's financial woes because when I wasn't at work, I was still busy making preparations for the mission field in Africa and preparing my heart for service.

At 7:00 in the morning on August 1, 2008, our mission team boarded a bus and headed for Atlanta, Georgia. After arriving safely in Atlanta, we boarded a plane for London and spent the next eight hours in flight. Upon touching down in

London, we experienced our first time change and a twelve-hour layover before boarding our next flight to Johannesburg, South Africa, and then nine more hours in the air. Once we made it to Johannesburg and through airport customs, we climbed into a semi-flatbed truck with an odometer reading almost 200,000.

Trying to make it to our temporary living quarters, we were driven on hideously dangerous roads with no street-lights and seemingly bottomless potholes cloaked by the darkness of the night. I was sleep deprived; I hadn't had a shower in the last thirty-six hours, and now I had the worst case of motion sickness I had experienced since I was an eight-year-old with a stomach full of cotton candy riding carnival rides at the state fair. I wondered what I had gotten myself into and jokingly asked God why he was torturing me.

Africa would create a hodgepodge of emotions for me; seeing desperation on some of the faces of the African women and small children and then expressing God's amazing love for them through an interpreter brought an irresistible spirit of compassion within me. Another time, I witnessed domineering African men exercising their authority over their subservient wives, which incensed me.

We spent time in orphanages and different villages, and on one particular occasion, we went into a village to conduct a women's ministry. Attempting to care for the African women the way Jesus showed His devotion to His disciples, we used our hand sanitizer and moistened face wipes to wash the feet of these women.

So he got up from the table, took off his robe, wrapped a towel around his waist, and poured water into a basin. Then he began to wash the disciples' feet and to wipe them with the towel he had around him. **(John 13:4–5, NLT)**

This experience was humbling for me and moved me to tears.

I had a secret, but this time, it had nothing to do with my sexual orientation. My birthday would fall on Sunday, August 10, while we were still in Africa. Always believing that it was better to give than receive, I made sure not to tell any of the other missionaries so they wouldn't plan anything special for me while we were out in the mission field. Instead, I went into Livingstone, Africa, a nearby town and purchased Tonga-language Bibles to have for the church we would be attending on Sunday. English was the primary language in Zambia; however, there were seventy spoken languages there, and Tonga was one of them. I wanted the Bibles I was giving to be written in one of their native languages.

On the morning of my birthday, I got up early and went out alone to pray and watch the sunrise while sitting on top of a hill. It was the most magnificent sunrise I had ever seen, and it was also the largest. The yellow, red, and orange tints contained in this seemingly perfectly round sun were so beautiful that the picture I took using my camera phone was of no comparison when I tried to describe God's grandeur to others through this photograph. I thanked God for the beautiful sunrise and then ran down the hill to get ready for church.

I handed out the Tonga Bibles to African women who came to the church from a nearby village, named Motto. It was amazing to be a part of the praise and worship during this service and to hear the preaching of God's Word giving a message of hope to many who had nothing more than their faith to sustain them. My birthday could not have been better, but at the end of the day, I ran back up the hill and watched the sunset. It was just as beautiful as the morning's sunrise. I thanked God for my life and for giving me such a remarkable birthday that I would always cherish.

Although I had idyllic reminiscences of my birthday, not everything in Africa would be a fond relic, as there would be a disturbing episode while we were working in one of the villages that would repeatedly haunt me. Before traveling to this particular village, we had prepared what I called "survival bags" for a couple hundred African villagers, and after teaching salvation through repentance of sin and having faith in Jesus Christ, we planned to end our message by having the villagers form a single-file line in order to hand out the survival bags. The bags contained an assortment of small-item tools, clothing, utensils, and hygiene supplies. As the natives spread the word that we were going to give the bags to them, more and more villagers appeared out of the thick brush. We had enough survival bags for two hundred, but I estimated that there were at least three hundred villagers waiting to receive.

As anticipation grew, the crowd broke out of single-file formation and began to rush to us. The dominant men were ripping the bags out of the hands of the African women, and the women were sending their small children back to get more bags. As our supply was quickly depleting, we were faced with a near-riot situation. Fearing that any one of us could be taken as a hostage, we threw down the remaining survival bags, grabbed our Bibles and teaching materials, and ran for our truck while our interpreters urged the crowd to stay back. As we pulled away, some of the natives were still chasing after our truck. It was a frightening experience, particularly for some of the younger missionaries in our group. I was apprehensive and mad at the same time.

I grieved angrily when I realized that our message of Jesus Christ took a backseat or may have been lost completely when the villagers saw us as modern-day Santa Clauses. I couldn't determine if the stampede by the villagers was out of a survival instinct or just pure greed, as they appeared to sacrifice their souls for a man-made gift bag. It was a disturbing image that I would see play out over and over again after I left Africa. Once I returned to the United States, I would continue to witness people sacrificing their souls to attain more and more, but the mission trip gave me an overwhelming appreciation for the blessings we took for granted that God gave us each day.

While standing in my kitchen, I was grateful to have a refrigerator with an abundance of food and bottled water inside. I was also grateful to have clean water and a hot shower at my disposal, and after riding in the barely operable truck in Africa, I was grateful for the transportation parked inside my garage. I realized that a lifestyle of self-centeredness had caused us to expect these things, but many would never indulge in these commodities simply because of circumstances.

It was September 2008, and I hadn't been back in the United States long when Chief Small promoted Ashley to lieutenant. Most everyone was flabbergasted because there was not a vacant lieutenant position available when she was promoted; many officers wondered what Ashley had done to obtain this rank. Chief Small had created a regulatory unit to handle nuisance complaints and then carved out a new lieutenant position to supervise the three-officer unit. With the stroke of a pen, the chief arranged a pay increase, a take-home car, and a personal office for the newly promoted lieutenant.

Finally, after filing my original complaint with the SCHAC in June 2007, I received a right-to-sue letter from the commission in January 2009, and their findings were adopted by the Equal Employment Opportunity Commission in February 2009. I remained employed at the police department but continued to look over my shoulder daily. With the illogical length of time it took to have my complaint investigated, it was a realistic assumption that a number of employees were likely forced to withdraw their complaints to the SCHAC or voluntarily leave their employment in order to relieve volatile work environments or to thwart retaliatory termination by their employers.

I was apprised of the fact that under federal law, a plaintiff had a right to file a lawsuit within ninety days of receiving the SCHAC findings, regardless of the outcome of the investigation, which made it difficult for me to appreciate the existence of this state agency. I actually felt my case was stuck in the mud throughout the entire process and their investigation ended up being completely irrelevant in the next step for my complaint. It was now time for me to make a decision whether or not to proceed with a lawsuit. The decision would ultimately be mine to make, and it was not a decision I took lightly. I would have to give Martha an answer soon, as each grain of sand passing through the hourglass added up to another day closer to the ninety-day deadline to file.

I would look to Dad and Magda for insight and support and once again, requested prayer from Sabina and Ma and Dad Hurt. Not knowing which way to turn, I diligently prayed for God to give me an answer as to what I should do. There were days and nights I didn't know how to pray or what to pray for but found encouragement in scripture:

And the Holy Spirit helps us in our distress. For we don't even know what we should pray for, nor how we should pray. But the Holy Spirit prays for us with groaning that cannot be expressed in words. And the Father who knows all hearts knows what the Spirit is saying, for the Spirit pleads for us believers in harmony with God's own will. **(Romans 8:26–27, NLT)**

Even though I continued to tap-dance around the issue of fully living for God and submitting to His will for my life, I still recognized that God was influential in me becoming a police officer, and I had no peace when I contemplated walking away from my lengthy career in law enforcement. After much prayer, I sent Martha a letter and enclosed a personal check, confirming that I had the support from my dad and those closest to me to proceed with the next step of the lawsuit. Filing a complaint and then going through a lawsuit was like climbing stairs with an obstacle course built into the staircase. I would take a few steps and then go over a hurdle and then take a few more steps. It didn't seem like I would ever reach the top floor, and there was no way around the obstacles and no elevator in sight.

Best Friend Sabina and me.

Ma Hurt & Me.

Father's Day weekend. From left to right
Michael, Michelle, Dad, Me, Carol.

Me washing the feet of the African women
during a mission trip to Zambia, Africa in
August 2008.

Uncle Grove.

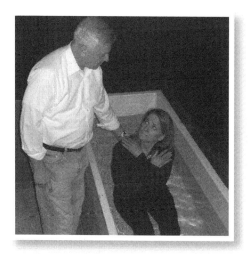

Pastor Phillip Miles counseling me on the importance of water baptism.

My water baptism at Christ Community Church, Conway, South Carolina, March 23, 2013.

15

RETIRE–REHIRE PROGRAM

In March 2009, while Martha began the outline for the legal verbiage of the lawsuit, Magda and I dug in our heels to research and write arguments for her. Having Magda's phenomenal mind to facilitate legal points of interest was invaluable to me as she and I did everything possible to make Martha's job easier. There are probably many trees that get cut down when a lawsuit is filed simply because of the amount of paperwork involved. Preparing arguments for my case and listing factual information in written format would be the first of many pages of legal red tape that Magda and I would painstakingly work on before handing the documents over to Martha on a silver platter. As the lawsuit foundation remained under construction for the next several weeks, the city was working on widening the entrance doors to a program that had started a few years earlier.

Before weighing the negative aspects, the retire-rehire program seemed like a good way to retain experienced,

knowledgeable, seasoned officers for the overall better-
ment of the department if their expertise would be applied.
However, in reality, the program was suffocating morale
and stifling the promotional process, and the effects of this
program would get worse as greed took over the souls of
many when they lined up to get their second slice of pie.
Officers not eligible to retire in order to participate in the
program called those participating "double-dippers" and
nicknamed them "ROAD" officers, meaning *retire on active
duty*, because they did more work before they retired than
when they returned to work under this program.

With the Police Officer Retirement System (PORS), an
officer with the required twenty-five years of service or an
employee who was at least fifty-five years of age could retire
and return to his or her job while collecting state retirement
benefits he or she had earned. Given the age or year requirement, most road-patrol officers were not eligible for the
retire-rehire program. State law stipulated that those workers retiring in order to begin participating in the retire-rehire
program must stay off the job for fifteen days after retiring,
but then the city allowed the employee to come back in his
or her current position and continue at his or her current
salary.

Because the police department had so many ranking
officers retire and come back, promotions were like dan-
gling a carrot in front of a donkey. Seated behind a desk in
an air-conditioned office, these retire-rehire participants did
nothing to help road-patrol shift coverage as shifts continued to operate with manpower at a bare minimum. This was
a scary reality considering the estimated daily and weekend

populations of Myrtle Beach swelled to epic proportions during the peak tourist season.

After overtime was cut, road-patrol officers were doing more with less as they struggled to make ends meet. Financial woes became apparent when word spread that an officer took a second job working at McDonald's and then another officer began working at Chick-Fil-A. Soon, road-patrol officers working part-time jobs became the norm while ranking officers continued double-dipping in the retire-rehire program. After the salary reduction from my demotion, I reluctantly began working an off-duty employment assignment as security for a movie theater to supplement lost income.

An intelligent solution for this retire-rehire fiasco would have been to allow those participating in the retire-rehire program to come back as police officers with the starting pay of a road-patrol officer. The department could then fill depleted road-patrol slots with well-trained veteran officers while saving thousands of dollars on salaries and allowing officers eligible for promotion to fill the vacancies of the ranking officers who had retired.

There were a number of palpable blemishes with this cash cow program to include the fact that there was no cap for the number of years anyone could participate in the program. Instead of city leaders hitting the reset button and implementing restrictions, they, too, jumped on board the same ship having a titanic effect on employee morale for those financially strapped and for those ineligible to participate. Now that the floodgates had opened, many avaricious ranking officers ineligible to retire on age or years of service were finding money to purchase service time to reach the twenty-five-year mark so they could retire and come back.

Having the knowledge that the city would soon officially be served with my lawsuit and not knowing the potential consequences for me, I considered purchasing service time— not to go ahead and retire but as a security blanket because of the unforeseen outcome of this litigation. I needed to get as close to twenty-five years as possible in the event I would have to involuntarily retire to avoid possibly being terminated in retaliation for filing the lawsuit.

I rolled over approximately thirty-three thousand dollars from my 401(k) plan into the South Carolina retirement system to purchase one year, four months, and five days of nonqualified service time. Dad was disappointed in my decision to buy the time and felt this made no sense. His belief was that a 401(k) plan was meant for retirement, not for ultimately buying freedom. Buying the time didn't get me to the required twenty-five-year mark, but the purchase would be another significant move as the rippling pond effect from the lawsuit was yet to come.

As the final draft of the lawsuit was nearing completion, Magda's internship was ending and she would be going back to Europe to utilize the special abilities God had given her to build her career as an attorney while working in a large international law firm in Warsaw, Poland. Despite the conflict of our relationship with our religious beliefs, we vowed to maintain our monogamous bond using webcam video chats and frequent-flier miles to travel back and forth for Christmas and Easter.

16

THE LAWSUIT

*When you go through deep waters and great trouble,
I will be with you. When you go through rivers of
difficulty, you will not drown! When you walk through
the fire of oppression, you will not be burned up; the
flames will not consume you.* **(Isaiah 43:2, NLT)**

My lawsuit, based on discrimination and retaliation, was filed on June 1, 2009, in the United States District Court, Florence, South Carolina, Division. Along with a request for a jury trial, Martha also asked the court for the following relief: "retroactive promotion to the rank of sergeant; back pay, front pay, lost employment benefits and raises, and interest thereon; liquidated damages equal to the amount of back pay owed to Plaintiff; compensatory damages for other economic losses directly and proximately caused by Defendant's unlawful conduct; compensatory damages for emotional distress, and other non-pecuniary losses; injunctive relief enjoining Defendants from engaging in discriminatory conduct in the future; actual and consequential damages; pre-judgment and post-judgment interest; enhancement to Plaintiff's actual, economic damages to account for any negative income tax consequences Plaintiff might sustain from receiving a damages award in a lump sum; attorney's fees, expert fees, and costs; and such further relief as the Court deems just and appropriate."

Despite any of Martha's relief requests, I remained faithful in praying for God's will to be done in this lawsuit, not mine. As a result of the lawsuit filing, by the first week of July 2009, the defense counsel countered back with their "First Interrogatories to Plaintiff and Defendant's First Continuing Request for Production of Documents and Things," which was nothing more than a scroll-sized laundry list of questions I was required to answer. Partial questions and information the defense demanded from me included: my last four years of income-tax returns; complete name, address, and telephone number of each physician, surgeon, psychologist, hospital, clinic, nurse, paramedic, hypnotist, pharmacist, or other health-care provider from whom I had obtained treatment, medications, or consultation; dates of consultations or treatment; the reason for treatment or consultation; diagnoses; names and dosages of medications prescribed or dispensed; current and former driver's license numbers; each name in full that I had ever used; each address I had ever had; the dates I used the addresses and the reason for each address change; past employment, including self-employment, with the full name, address, and telephone number of each employer, dates of employment, description of job or position held, wages or salary received, the number of hours worked per week, and disciplinary action taken and the reason the employment ended; all current and past enrollment in any educational or training institutions, including the full name and address of each institution attended, dates of enrollment, major course of study, dates of certificates and degrees obtained, and status while enrolled (i.e., part-time, resident, commuter, correspondent).

I was utterly overwhelmed to have to provide this type of information, and because of the Rules of Civil Procedure, I was required to give them this information in writing and under oath within thirty days. I speculated that the city's legal team was going to try to paint me as a psychotic gold-digger, while attempting to intimidate me with their lengthy information demands. I had nothing to hide, but I did find the demands for this information to be an enormous invasion of privacy. Suddenly, Brenda Christy was put under a magnifying glass, and I thought to myself, *I'm the one who filed the lawsuit; why is my life being turned completely upside down?*

While I worked feverishly to provide the infinite amount of required information to Martha in an expeditious manner, more atrocious news would be on the way when several city employees, including me, learned that our longevity with the city was as beneficial as a toy without batteries for a kid on Christmas Day. The city announced, without remorse, that they were reneging on a promise they made several years earlier when they gave their word to continue to pay health insurance premiums for employees who retired with at least twenty years of continuous service. The news was a shock to us all, but to show their sportsmanship, the city announced their interpretation of a compatible benefit in the Retiree Health Reimbursement Account (RHRA).

The newly developed account was for employees who retired after July 1, 2009, with twenty years' (the last ten years consecutive) service with the city; they would have one hundred thousand dollars in a RHRA to be used for insurance premiums. If/when the RHRA was depleted, the employee might still participate in the plan by paying the monthly premium out of his or her own pocket; however, in 2012, these premiums were almost seven hundred dollars a month. Ouch!

When retirees reached sixty-five, Medicare started and they automatically came off the city's health plan. So hypothetically, if the employee began employment with the city in his or her early twenties, he or she would be eligible to retire in his or her late forties and still have roughly sixteen years before becoming eligible for Medicare. It didn't take a rocket scientist to figure out the funds in the city's created (RHRA) were a drop in the bucket. I interpreted the broken promise as city administrators sacrificing their souls, and when I and the other longevity employees cried foul, the city whispered, "The promise was never put in writing."

Even after I met my required deadlines for providing the information for the "production of documents and things" for the defense, the exchange of information through this motion-of-discovery process took on a life of its own. Swapping evidence between Martha and the defense counsel would take yet another year off the calendar. There would be no crystal ball to tell me how long the legal sequence would take or how much money fighting this lawsuit would cost me and my dad. The process would prove to be a painful one.

Every time I went to my post office box to get my mail, it was like going to have a meeting with the Grim Reaper because there was always a bill for attorney fees or more legal paperwork that needed my immediate attention. As I tried to gain traction while climbing the slippery slope of this litigation process, it appeared that the city was galloping effortlessly; after all, the city had deep pockets and endless resources to handle the costs of litigation, such as insurance coverage, a team of legal counselors, and a number of administrative assistants at their disposal. This warfare with the city often made me feel like Daniel in the lion's den, but without the miraculous ending.

As weeks passed, due dates for legal fees continued each month; Dad, with his analytical mind, became increasingly impatient and wanted to see results for the thousands of dollars he was investing. There was no gray area with Dad; the city was wrong in what they had done to his daughter, and he expected a prompt resolution to his daughter's suffering. It became regrettably clear to me that the lawsuit was beginning to affect my family. Dad became very pessimistic concerning the fairness of the legal process; he saw the underdog position I was in and agonized, knowing he was unable to pull me from the lion's teeth.

There were many arguments between me and my siblings over the emotional and financial burden the lawsuit was having on our dad. At the same time, Dad and my stepmom were struggling with differing opinions on their financial obligation to me for what was ultimately my battle to fight. I saw the fabric of what I called family being stretched and unraveled. Going back home to West Virginia to celebrate my dad's October birthday or Father's Day became distant memories, and the effects of the lawsuit continued at the Thanksgiving and Christmas dinner table where my place setting sat bare in my absence.

After establishing Myrtle Beach as my second home, I had formed some of my own holiday traditions, and each year, I would hand out Christmas cookies and give my sincere best wishes for the New Year to my neighbors. After repeating this tradition for at least a decade, I decided Christmas 2009 would be no different. Since my Christmas plans did not include going to West Virginia, I was excited Magda would fly in from Europe for the holidays.

When exchanging Christmas cheer with my neighbor Elsa, she told me, "Don't play with God." Of course, Elsa was referring to my relationship with Magda, a relationship she thoroughly disapproved of because of her own religious beliefs. I don't remember the entire conversation, but in a rude manner, I told her people didn't chose whom they fell in love with and she should mind her own business. I challenged her spiritual authority over me with scripture: *You, then, why do you judge your brother? Or why do you look down on your brother? For we will all stand before God's judgment seat.* **(Romans: 14:10, NIV)**

I didn't realize at the time God was speaking to me through Elsa, but it would become very apparent to me when Elsa's faith would be tested as she would later endure a serious health crisis.

17

GOOD AND EVIL

While officers were ringing in the New Year and hoping for a prosperous 2010, I was praying for a trial date to be set, as the city was premeditating a full-court press strategy to present to a magistrate judge hoping to have summary judgment granted to them. After all, summary judgment arguments were where the rubber met the road. A judge's ruling would determine if the case would proceed to trial or be tossed out of court.

Before all the confetti could be swept off the streets of Manhattan's Time Square, doom and gloom would settle into the atmosphere of the police department as overtime was slashed completely and tuition reimbursement was eliminated, as well as any across-the-board pay increases.

These imposed sacrifices did not appear to have much effect on the retire-rehire participants or the command staff. Collectively, this group had a propensity to flaunt their peacock feathers while repeating the "be glad you have a job" message to the road-patrol officers. Road-patrol officers, in turn, labeled this type of posturing as "drinking the Kool-Aid," meaning as long as they drank the tainted Kool-Aid, they would walk around creating a facade of "we're all one big, happy family" even though the peacocks were the only ones happy.

Morale continued to plummet and officers began sacrificing their souls any way possible to get ahead. A self-serving attitude became predominant as officers quit looking out for each other and went into survival mode. Since there was no money allotted for overtime and raises through promotions were few and far between, off-duty employment opportunities that would help supplement income for the road officers became the hot-ticket item. Off-duty jobs provided a small amount of relief for the financial woes the road-patrol officers endured until Chief Small made a senseless decision to allow the command staff officers (including the retire-rehire participates) to put their name in the hat to work these extra details.

This proclamation from Small dramatically shrank the probability that road-patrol officers would be selected for these extra-income opportunities. There was, however, a policy in place for off-duty employment opportunities, but the legitimacy of this policy became contentious when the same command staff officers were continually seen working several of the off-duty jobs.

Unfortunately, as I experienced the inexcusable tactics the city was using in the litigation process and witnessed the changes in the attitudes of the officers, I sometimes perceived some people as mean-spirited and often times just plain evil. It brought to mind a quote I had read by Dr. Martin Luther King Jr.: "There is some good in the worst of us and some evil in the best of us. When we discover this, we are less prone to have our enemies." As I carefully tried to balance Dr. King's quote between my own good and evil discernment of others, I prayed to see the best in everyone, but instead, I expected the worst.

As Martha and I were working on scheduling a meeting location to hold our depositions and a date for these sworn statements to be obtained, I went to Europe to spend Easter with Magda. We were in Germany on April 10, 2010, when we received the horrific news that Lech Kaczynski, the then Polish president had been killed in a plane crash, along with his wife, Maria, and dozens of the country's top political and military leaders, as they traveled to Western Russia to the site of the Katyn Massacre, a mass murder of Polish intellectuals, politicians, and military officers by the Soviets seventy years ago.

Magda and I wasted no time in taking the next train back to Warsaw to join thousands of grieving Poles. Masses of people formed outside the presidential palace and inside cathedrals for prayer and mourning, as many were still healing from the death of the Polish Pope John Paul II just five years earlier.

As Poland's calamity brought eerie reflections to me of America's grief in the aftermath of the 9/11 tragedy, I saw the hopelessness of lost souls in the eyes of many as we passed in the streets and church sanctuaries throughout

Europe. And just as in the United States, it was apparent from my conversations that many of those lost souls had a thirst to know Jesus, but disappointingly, for reasons undisclosed to me, quite a few gave the impression that they only held a hymnal or a Bible in their hands during the traditional Christmas or Easter church services.

It became apparent to me that the despondency of many Americans and Europeans was due to cultures lacking faith in Christ. Poland's latest tragedy would add to the desperation of many in Europe. Unfortunately, as I witnessed this suffering during my time in Europe, I did not have the aptitude to sufficiently communicate that our refuge was in knowing Jesus Christ as scripture tells us. *The LORD is good, a refuge in times of trouble. He cares for those who trust in him.* **(Nahum 1:7, NIV)**

During one of my stays in Poland, I spent time talking with Magda's best friend, Maja. My inadequacy to properly share my belief in Christ would become more apparent during a lengthy conversation we shared. As we bounced from topic to topic, we touched on cultural differences and similarities women share when they mistakenly define the value of their soul in their physical appearance and beauty. It seemed that because of society, many European women were programmed to judge their own success when, through extreme measures, they were able to go from a size-four waistline to a size zero. As Maja expressed her desire to find a soul mate, there was an underlying fallacy that being beautiful and wearing designer labels were keys to attracting a man with husband qualities. It was hard for me to convey to Maja that God was not a magician or a genie in a bottle, but He was available to all who sought to know Him. *I sought the LORD, and he answered me and delivered me from all my fears.* **(Psalms 34:4, ESV)**

As we continued to chat candidly about our belief in God, we debated the best way to establish a personal relationship with Jesus and whether there was any truth that being a good person by doing good deeds would "win" us a place in heaven. Because my Bible was still in my unpacked suitcase and I was a nominal Christian at the time, I could not answer Maja precisely, so those questions remained unsettled. Our conversation became permanently tattooed in my mind and remained with me long after I returned to the United States.

As I subconsciously grappled with my nominal Christian status, I searched for scriptures relating to our query. **Ephesians 4:5, (NLT)** says, *There is only one Lord, one faith, one baptism* and **James 4:8, (NLT)** says, *Draw close to God, and God will draw close to you. Wash your hands, you sinners; purify your hearts, you hypocrites.* As for doing good deeds, *"Can we boast, then, that we have done anything to be accepted by God? No, because our acquittal is not based on our good deeds. It is based on our faith."* **(Romans 3:27, NLT)**

A short time after I returned to the United States to resume my work schedule, Martha notified me that depositions had been scheduled to begin on June 23, 2010, in Myrtle Beach. The scheduling order put City Manager Todd Long as the first to give a sworn testimony that day, at which time he recalled meeting with me and giving his approval of my demotion by Chief Small.

Q: Did you review any documents before you signed off on the demotion?

A: No.

Q: Do you recall what information was given to you when you approved the demotion of Brenda Christy?

A: Not specifically.

Q: Okay. What information did you go on when you made that decision?

A: What normally would happen and I assume happened in this case is that Chief Small called me or came to see me. I can't remember which, explained the situation, probably asked questions to make sure I didn't have any questions that needed to be answered or they had overlooked something and at the end of the conversation, obviously approved this course of action.

Q: Do you remember what he explained to you, what he told you?

A: I really don't.

Q: And you had met with Brenda March 5, correct?

A: Yes, 2007.

Q: Right, and this is May 20 something in 2007. Maybe six weeks later, correct?

A: Yes.

Q: And between the time she met with you and the time Chief Small was calling you, you had not gotten back to Brenda or looked into anything she complained about, correct?

A: Correct.

Chief Small was deposed on June 28, 2010. During his sworn testimony, he was questioned on a number of topics, including the investigation completed on me in February 2007 and my meeting with the city manager in March 2007.

Q: Okay. Do you know whether or not Brenda Christy met with the city manager at any time during the spring of 2007?

A: Yes.

Q: How did you know that she had met with him?

A: He told me.

Q: Okay. Did y'all have a discussion about her situation?

A: I'm sure we did.

Q: Do you recall what that was about?

A: Just a conversation about her dissatisfaction with the way she was being treated and that she felt like she was being discriminated against and, you know, we were retaliating against her and, you know, and basically the city manager said he listened to her, her side of the story and he was...he had been kept abreast of the situation that was ongoing that we were having, and that was it. I didn't hear anything more about it for a little while until, you know, probably about May.

Q: And what did you hear in May?

A: I mean that's when I went back to him and we discussed the demotion.

Sergeant Ashley Prior was one of several officers in Chief Small's command staff to give sworn affidavits against me after the lawsuit was filed. Concerning the drug complaint that my officers did not handle correctly, prompting the investigation on me in February 2007, Sergeant Prior made the following statement in her affidavit.

All officers in "B" bracket came to me, very distraught about the incident as well as continuing issues they were having with Christy. The officers said they were not sure what to do as they had already attempted to talk with

Christy. Officer Devericks explained to me that he was surprised about Christy's reaction to a case. He said they attempted to explain the situation to Christy, but she would not listen. Devericks further stated that Christy kept repeating herself and antagonizing Officer Faas by using inappropriate language and raising her voice. Devericks said he felt she was trying to instigate not only a verbal argument but possibly a physical one because she was up in their faces about the issue and would not give them any time to explain. Faas said Christy was extremely animated throwing her hands up in the air as well as being daunting.

Not only did the tape-recorded statements from these subordinates and final report by Lieutenant Heiden refute Prior's sworn affidavit, Chief Small's sworn deposition testimony contradicted her statement when he recalled the investigation.

Q: Do you recall there being some sort of internal investigation of Brenda Christy during February of 2007 regarding some complaints made by her subordinates?

A: An internal investigation?

Q: Or any type of investigation?

A: I think if I recall that supervisors were inquiring about the complaints the officers were making.

Q: All right. Who conducted that investigation?

A: I think the supervisors of that unit.

Q: How was it conducted?

A: Talk to the officers, find out what their problem is, and try to resolve it.

Q: Was it resolved?

A: If I'm not mistaken, the initial complaint was there was a dispute with some officers over an action that she took as a supervisor or some directives she gave. They were not real happy with that action. As I recall, it was...that initial part was there was not a whole lot to it. There was nothing to support their allegations that she was doing anything wrong in that particular instance and that particular case that they were complaining about.

Another sworn affidavit was obtained from my former captain Bob Franklin. In his affidavit, Franklin stated that he had "opposed consideration of Christy for promotion based on her ongoing poor judgment, lack of honesty, and apparent inability to set a good example for other officers." Bob Franklin was mentioned in Chief Small's deposition because of his email correspondence with the chief concerning my demotion.

Q: All right. And this email from Bob Franklin, where is Bob Franklin now?
A: Bob Franklin is still in Myrtle Beach.
Q: Okay. Is he employed by the police department?
A: No, he's not.
Q: And what is the reason he resigned?
A: He resigned in lieu of termination.

Ironically, in August 2009, Captain Franklin was arrested and charged by North Carolina Highway Patrol for driving while intoxicated, open container violation, and reckless driving. These charges were widely reported in the local broadcast and print news media. Another sworn affidavit was submitted by Captain Dale Knisely. Captain Dale Knisely admitted immediately that "...I have not directly supervised or dealt with Brenda Christy…" and that his only knowledge was derived "…from communications with others…"

The affidavits offered against me were from high-ranking officers directly or indirectly involved in Chief Small's command staff. They sacrificed their souls because they were obliged to support the chief's agenda or were beholden to the chief for allowing them to resign rather than be fired and for being permitted to participate in the retire–rehire program. Fascinatingly, the city did not offer even one affidavit from a subordinate I supervised during the year of my demotion who they claimed was dissatisfied with my supervisory skills or who allegedly wanted to transfer because of my supervision.

18

BARRACUDAS

fter rereading all the sworn affidavits against me and the numerous piles of documents the city's legal team had engineered to persuade a judge to throw out my case, I felt like a small fish being chased upstream by a school of barracudas. August 2010, I spent hours scouring the city's rebuttals and arguments for my claims of discrimination and retaliation, finding blatant mistruths and misrepresentation of facts. While reviewing the city's written response to the SCHAC for my discrimination and retaliation claim, I discovered they made an allegation that I forwarded a written complaint to Chief City Judge Janice Walter regarding Judge Walter's handling of a case several years prior and that I was disciplined because I sent the letter without my supervisor's knowledge.

Unaware of any such letter or of any disciplinary action taken against me, I went and reviewed my personnel file and could not find a copy of the letter or the corrective action.

I also spoke to Judge Walter's administrative secretary, who said she handled all mail and interoffice envelopes for Judge Walter, but she had no knowledge of any such letter. Always having a good rapport with Judge Walter, I made an appointment to meet with her in chambers, at which time she could not recall receiving any written complaint from me. Judge Walter became exasperated as she expressed to me her discontentment with her name being used arbitrarily without her knowledge or consent by the city in the SCHAC response. After brainstorming, she and I were of the conclusion the written complaint I supposedly sent to her never existed.

Judge Walter, an African-American woman over the age of forty, said she wanted to provide a sworn affidavit on my behalf for the fictitious letter and the misrepresentation of her name by the city. Judge Walter continued to exhibit her agitation during our meeting and expressed her desire to convey the truth to my attorney. Judge Walter then instructed me to "Get Martha on the phone." As we sat in her chambers during a brief phone conversation, Judge Walter informed Martha she was furnishing an affidavit to her and she would meet with City Manager Long and Chief Small the following day to confront them and also to advise them of her intention. The next day, Judge Walter called me into her chambers and informed me of her reproach of Long and Small. She stated after little response from either of them, they both left her chambers, red-faced.

Days after Judge Walter met with Long and Small and after additional consultation with city officials, Judge Walter never provided the affidavit she had promised, and without delay, the city's defense counsel contacted Martha via formal memorandum to advise her that Judge Walter wanted no further contact with me or her. I was not privy to the conversation Judge Walter had with city officials; however, my intuition tells me she sacrificed her soul to protect her $110,000 salary and fringe benefits by not providing the affidavit, as I believe what's in your soul is what you place significance on and what in turn directs your behavior.

This was an unforeseen backhand to my cheek by Judge Walter, but I would have to turn the other cheek as I continued to gather documents and affidavits in support of my case, helping to tweak our written arguments in order for a magistrate judge to deny summary judgment to the city so I could proceed to trial. These were nerve-racking times for me, but I found inspiration watching a handful of Christian athletes professing their faith both on and off the playing field and by spending time in scripture and on my knees in prayer.

I was prone to thinking the Bible was too hard to understand and always carelessly thumbed through it looking for divine intervention. This approach made as much sense as speeding in rush-hour traffic, blindfolded, hoping not to wreck. As I got over my reluctance for reading the Bible by removing my blindfold, I began to find meaning in God's Word while seeing the misery within my soul. *Open my eyes to see the wonderful truths in your law.* **(Psalms 119:18, NLT)**

As I was learning to trust God for help, officers' grumbling over pay and working conditions continued to get louder and louder. Regardless of their complaints and cries for help, in September 2010, Chief Small's drumbeat drowned them out when he gave a quote to Steve Porter, a journalist for a local newspaper, "We've been doing our part trying to explain to the officers that they should be happy that you have a job." Wow! I thought, as I read the chief's insensible comment in the article.

There was an obvious lack of a human element within the department from when I started my police career in 1987 until that day, as it became an "us versus them" mentality. Briefing was replaced by technology and social media, which also added to the level of frustration for the officers. It was common practice for supervisors to monitor their subordinates through their Facebook and Twitter accounts, as well as their blogs, or by texting them from their smartphones, rather than having face-to-face conversations.

In November 2010, it was hard to overlook the narcissistic appearance that shadowed City Manager Todd Long and Chief Wade Small as they both began participating in the retire-rehire program, adding insult to injury for officers barely making ends meet. Long retired and came back to his $160,000 salary, and soon thereafter, Small retired and stepped back into his $125,000 salary, while they both began drawing their retirement benefits! The news for the officers regarding Small's participation in the retire-rehire program was as welcome as a piece of gum stuck on the bottom of their work boot. There is truth to the saying "What goes around comes around." In Small's demotion letter to me, he wrote that I was unable to gain the respect of my subordinates when, in fact, he lost all respect as our commander and chief when he retired and came back under this program.

Trying to escape the disgruntlement of the work arena, I began preparing my heart for gratitude as the Thanksgiving holiday approached, but regrettably, I would still face another Thanksgiving without Dad. Elsa, my neighbor, stopped over and she once again told me, "Don't play with God." After she left, I felt sick on my stomach and became very nauseated. I remembered a quote from Dr. Charles Stanley, "God loves you the way you are, but He loves you enough not to leave you the way you are." I felt God convicting me about my relationship with Magda, and this night became a defining moment for me. I was tired of being a lukewarm Christian, straddling the fence and just going through the religious motions, when I knew scripture:

Do you not know that the wicked will not inherit the Kingdom of God? Do not be deceived: Neither the sexually immoral nor idolaters nor adulterers nor male prostitutes nor homosexual offenders nor thieves nor the greedy nor drunkards nor slanderers nor swindlers will inherit the kingdom of God. **(1 Corinthians 6:9–10 NIV)**

Sabina and Ma and Dad Hurt never viewed me as damaged goods but also conceded that they had always prayed that I would repent of my sins and turn my life completely to Christ.

I realized no matter how many times I had previously been convicted, I sacrificed my own soul as collateral to keep my relationship with Magda, bartering anything before God in prayer. Normally, Magda would come to the United States for Christmas, but I was besieged at work and she was making triumphant gains at her law firm. Her new schedule demands kept her in Europe for the holiday. We were growing apart because of my conviction and her ascent up the career ladder; therefore, before the New Year, we ended our relationship as we knew it, but pinky swore that we would remain good friends. The year 2011 would be a year of uncertainty for me as I continued to pray to overcome a summary judgment decision and for a trial date to be set, all while trying to find peace in my choice to regain the value of my soul through repentance.

In February 2011, I began attending a nondenominational church that I quickly became fond of. The church held its services in a dilapidated building in a less-than-desirable part of downtown Myrtle Beach. Nevertheless, the pastor had a faithful group of thirty or forty members making up the congregation, mostly of what appeared to be poor and unemployed individuals. Those of us who were working looked to be part of the lower-middle-class or middle-class workforce. There was no glitz or glamour walking through the house of worship doors there, but despite the decaying building, I fell in love with the people making up this church. I felt my giving spirit could be best used in this type of environment, helping to remind me of one of my favorite scriptures: *There are three things that will endure—faith, hope, and love— and the greatest of these is love."* **(1 Corinthians 13:13, NLT)** Moreover, this scripture provided solace for me while the ubiquitous lawsuit wrecking ball continued to tear down my wall of buoyancy.

19

CHAMPIONS

By April 2011, the pain in my left foot was unbearable, and I would be unable to postpone surgery any longer. While still awaiting a summary judgment decision, I had a very complex and painful foot surgery. Although my orthopedic surgeon warned me of the challenges and difficulties I would face during my recovery period, I never imagined not walking for almost three months and having countless days and nights of unmanageable and unbearable pain.

My intention was to return to work as soon as my doctor released me from his care even though on July 7, 2011, I became eligible to retire as a result of rolling over my 401(k) into the state retirement system. I was still out on medical leave, still immobilized from my foot operation, and anxiously anticipating a summary judgment ruling any day. As I continued to recuperate and remained dependent on a wheelchair and crutches to navigate through my daily routine, God continued to convict me in other areas of weakness in my life. For me, having physical limitations made temporary seem like forever, and somberly through my disability, I came to the startling awareness, each day, thousands of people would unfortunately find out their fate as their journey would be abruptly stopped or altered permanently through an automobile or motorcycle collision, illness, natural disaster, by-product of war, birth defect, or a freak accident.

This recently acquired awareness triggered a recollection of a robbery that occurred one tragic November morning in 2009 while I was on duty. Myrtle Beach Police responded to a department store parking lot after a seventy-three-year-old woman had her purse snatched by an unidentified female suspect. Upon hearing screams for help, an innocent shopper, Brenda Dewitt-Williams, sprang into action and chased down the perpetrator. While attempting an escape, the perpetrator got into her car, started the engine, and ran over the courageous Dewitt-Williams, dragging her like a rag doll before her helpless body fell from the fleeing automobile. The perpetrator would eventually be arrested in Georgia and following her court appearance, began serving a particularly lenient prison sentence.

After fighting for her life and then completing months of painful and agonizing physical therapy at a spinal center, the prognosis was still the same; this mother of two, still in the prime of her life, would be paralyzed from the waist down and confined to a wheelchair. While recovering from my foot surgery, I had the pleasure of visiting this extraordinary woman. I was inspired by her faith in Jesus Christ and her lack of regret for getting involved. There was something remarkable within her soul that caused her to risk her own life for a complete stranger. After praying with this heroine, my immobilization from foot surgery became insignificant to me.

My uncle Ralph Grover Christy then came to mind. He was better known by his nieces and nephew as "Grove." Grove was born with cerebral palsy, a debilitating disorder that affects muscle control and coordination. Growing up in the same town where my uncle lived gave me countless opportunities to interact with him. Throughout my childhood and into my adolescence, I remember my uncle relying on a cane to assist him standing and stabilizing his movements as he would walk. With each passing year, my uncle's mobility decreased significantly in his lower extremities.

As I entered into college, it was necessary for Grove to give up his cane for a sturdier, more reliable walker. Nevertheless, he continued to live on his own. Grove lived in a low-income apartment complex next to the community college I attended. I remember the ritual of me going to his apartment in between classes. He was always so happy to see me, but I was more preoccupied with taking a nap in order to nurse a hangover from the night before. Throughout my frequent visits, I remember his legs were not supporting his body. It became very cumbersome for him as he would drag them behind when moving around in his one-bedroom apartment with his walker.

I loved my uncle, but I didn't remember doing anything to help make his life easier for him, such as washing his dishes, changing the sheets on his bed, or vacuuming his apartment.

Each new birthday for my uncle brought on more restrictions to his mobility. He abandoned his walker and with great hesitation began utilizing a wheelchair; however, he still maintained the sunny disposition for which he was known.

Somewhere around 2002, it was evident that Grove could no longer complete daily activities, such as bathing unassisted and maintaining the normal upkeep of his apartment. Reluctantly, he was moved into a nursing home. Almost a decade later, my uncle was nearly bedridden, but his ability to be content in even the worst situations amazed me and reminded me of a Bible verse:

Not that I was ever in need, for I have learned how to get along happily whether I have much or little. I know how to live on almost nothing or with everything. I have learned the secret of living in every situation, whether it is with a full stomach or empty, with plenty or little. For I can do everything with the help of Christ who gives me the strength I need. **(Philippians 4:11–13, NLT)**

Even with assistance from Dad and other family members, I couldn't help but wonder how my uncle lived disabled for so many years on his own. In the time I spent as a disabled person, I realized that amenities, such as motorized shopping carts, handicap bathroom stalls with arm rails, debit cards, drive-through windows, cell phones, and having contact with compassionate people were a necessity, but a lot of these services were unavailable for my uncle as he struggled for years with his disability.

At a difficult period during my recovery, I had an eye-opening experience during a routine trip to Walmart to get first-aid supplies. Once inside, I unpredictably realized that I was unable to walk down the long, narrow aisles or carry more than one or two items while on crutches. I left my crutches at the front entrance and discreetly got into a motorized cart. I quickly noticed that most of the shoppers were desensitized to the motorized cart I was operating as people darted around me as if I was holding them up. No one allowed me to get in front of them at the checkout line; no one offered to carry my bagged items to my car, and it was totally out of the question for anyone to help me get an item off the shelf, even if it was completely out of my reach while seated in a two-foot-high motorized cart.

When I was out in public, whether I was in a motorized cart at the grocery store or utilizing my crutches in a crowded parking lot, when people saw me, most of them appeared to sacrifice their souls by looking the other way and pretending not to see me as I struggled while moving closer in their direction. It was poetic justice for the lack of respect I showed for my uncle growing up. I was convicted for my lack of empathy toward my uncle, and I prayed for forgiveness. Ironically, while still on crutches, I drove from Myrtle Beach, South Carolina, to West Virginia. I hobbled into my uncle's room at the nursing home, and with tears of regret raining down my face, I begged his forgiveness. True to his compassionate nature, he quickly let me know how happy he was to see me and immediately forgave me for my transgression. I was thankful for the conviction that brought me to my senses and grateful my uncle forgave me. Indubitably, my uncle, Brenda Dewitt-Williams, and all men, women, and children with disabilities, who are forced to live in a sometimes unkind world, are the true champions of life.

Returning home from my trip to see my uncle would mark almost three months since my foot had touched the ground, but after analyzing x-rays, my orthopedic doctor cheerfully gave me the thumbs-up sign, indicating my foot had finally healed, and I was ready for physical therapy. I was exuberant to once again walk, a blessing many of us take for granted. As I celebrated my freedom of movement, I vigilantly kept one ear bent, expecting to hear the magistrate judge's recommendation to affirm or deny summary judgment soon.

20

JELLYFISH

t was the end of July 2011 when I received the report
and recommendation from United States Magistrate
Judge Timothy B. Roberts III, recommending
summary judgment be awarded to the city. As I read through
his lopsided interpretation of facts for my case, I noticed his
unfair emphasis on the discipline given to me as far back
as 1993, while he discounted my "substantially exceeds
expectations" evaluation the year I was demoted. Despite the
contradictions in the deposition testimonies, Judge Roberts
gave credence to the sworn affidavits provided against me
while refuting affidavits in my favor. I provided to the court
an affidavit from retired Police Sergeant Harvey Raines.

I am fifty-two years old. I was employed by the Myrtle
Beach Police Department from 1982 until I retired as a
Sergeant in 2007. I worked directly with Brenda Christy
as her supervisor for several years, and I had professional

contact with her during the years when I was not her supervisor. I have personal knowledge of and am competent to testify as to the matters stated herein.

I supervised Investigator Brenda Christy on the midnight shift patrol during approximately 2002 and 2003. We were both transferred to the day shift patrol around 2003 through 2005. I believe I also supervised her during subsequent years, even up to 2007.

I had many opportunities to observe her job performance, and I gave her high marks on her evaluations. During part of the time that I supervised Inv. Christy, I reported to Wade Small as my Captain. After Small was promoted to Chief, I reported to Captain Veit. Both Small and Veit signed off on and gave their approval to my favorable evaluations of Inv. Christy.

I recall that I remarked on one of my performance evaluations that Inv. Christy was at the pinnacle of her career, and that she should be in line to become Sergeant—or words to that effect. I believe that she had the leadership skills and experience to hold the rank of Sergeant. In fact, if I had the ability to choose a co-supervisor to work with I would choose Brenda Christy.

I recall that Inv. Christy at times had approximately 14 or 15 officers under her command. No officer ever came to me requesting to transfer out from under her supervision.

I found Inv. Christy to be a very direct and truthful person. She never lied to me; I could trust her and I depended heavily on her as a supervisor. I do know that if she or anyone else in the Myrtle Beach Police Department ever lied, they would have been fired immediately by Chief Small.

Inv. Christy was very knowledgeable about police work, and quite diligent. She did not have the typical "female people skills," however, I think that law enforcement is a "man's world' and sometimes females have to work harder to prove themselves. Sometimes she could come down hard on the officers, but that's what it took to get the job done; it wasn't a bad thing. I didn't have any problem working with her. With our personalities, it was like we played "good cop / bad cop" and it worked for us. It was very effective.

Inv. Christy was always challenged to prove herself. The City always said, "We are family." They "talked the talk," but they didn't "walk the walk."

I believe, based upon my experience, the decisions to deny Inv. Christy a promotion to Sergeant and to demote her were not justified by her record of service.

Judge Roberts was still able to use Harvey's affidavit negatively against me by plucking out words to form sentences for his opinion: "perhaps at times did not display good 'people skills,' and seemed to come off strong," all while

disregarding Harvey's affidavit in its entirety. Given the circumstances of Chief Small denying promotions to me on two
separate occasions, the burden to prove a *prima facie* case
in my eyes had been met in that I was a member of a protected group; I applied for the positions in question; I was
qualified for the positions; and I was rejected for promotion
when the positions were awarded to younger, less-qualified
male employees. Judge Roberts cited that "the Promotional
Process Policy allowed Chief Small to choose from any of
the top three candidates in the pool and further noted that
Courts do not sit as super personnel departments second
guessing employers' qualifications."

When considering my retaliation claim, Judge Roberts
failed to even scratch the surface or examine the instances
that were mentioned in the lawsuit in which I raised my concern about discrimination in my chain of command subsequent to the 2002 sexual harassment incident and particularly
within the few months and weeks just prior to my demotion in 2007. Instead, Judge Roberts focused solely upon the
2002 incident where I reported the sexual harassment of a
coworker, and he found that I could not establish a causal
connection between the 2002 report and the 2007 demotion, even though the 2002 sexual harassment was only the
beginning of the continuum for the discrimination and retaliation I endured. Judge Roberts's opinion in his report and
recommendation was as transparent as a jellyfish, and just
as a jellyfish has no heartbeat, I found no heart in his words.
And if you get too close to a jellyfish, you will get stung, just
as the words coming off the pages of Judge Roberts's report
and recommendation stung me.

Judge Roberts did not view evidence in a light most favorable to me, but his job was to make a recommendation to the court. The responsibility to make a final determination remained with the court. The court could accept, reject, or modify, in whole or in part, the recommendation of the magistrate judge or might recommit the matter with instructions. I would rely again on everyone in my prayer circle to commit this to prayer while Martha and I appealed Judge Roberts's recommendation. Our concerns would be reviewed by the United States district judge.

With my relationship with Magda now fully established as friends, I was making noticeable efforts to rededicate my life to Christ when my neighbor Elsa began making regular stops to my house to check on my progress from the foot surgery and get prayer requests concerning my lawsuit. At the end of September 2011, Elsa stopped by to inform me that she had been diagnosed with small-cell carcinoma, a type of highly malignant cancer that most commonly arose within the lung. Strangely, Elsa's cancer was detected in her femur, esophagus, and liver, and while the prognosis was dismal, this devout Catholic proclaimed her faith in the Lord and vowed to fight the disease regardless of the number of chemotherapy or radiation treatments her body had to endure.

I went to church as usual on Sunday morning and committed to pray for Elsa's recovery from this terrible disease. During the church service, my pastor could hardly contain himself as he announced that we as a church had found a newer building to lease in a better area of town. He explained this new building would need many renovations to meet code enforcement regulations and the congregation would have to pull together to complete much of the work in order to keep down construction costs. Enthusiastically, the congregation committed to the task and looked forward to what the future would bring for our church.

My church and constant prayer became my sources of strength and encouragement, which helped me get through difficult times, such as the day I spoke with Investigator Dana Pearson in the Street Crimes office. After the city had won the opinion of Judge Roberts, they considered his decision a slam dunk, and supervisors ordered Officer Randy Alliston to remove my pictures off the wall and clean out my belongings from my desk in the cubicle from which I worked. Pearson then gave me my belongings in a cardboard box, and though I had not retired or resigned and I had not been fired, I was not given a valid reason why my personal belongings had been removed from my workspace.

However, I would get a reprieve from the opposition in October 2011, when I received the opinion and order from District Judge J. Melinda Chapels regarding her review of Judge Roberts's report and recommendation. Judge Chapels concurred with parts of Judge Roberts's opinion but conceded that he failed to consider or address any of the reports of discrimination that I made after 2002. Specifically, no opinion was reflected by Judge Roberts regarding my complaint in March 2007 to City Manager Todd Long or my March 2007 meeting with Chief Small and for my complaint to Lieutenant McFarland in May 2007.

Judge Chapels recommitted the matter to Judge Roberts with instructions to consider my claims of retaliation in light of these reports of discrimination. At this stage, Martha and the city's legal team had previously provided all written arguments and information pertaining to these retaliation claims to Judge Roberts, and it should have been just a matter of him reviewing these documents and applying the law to support or deny a summary judgment ruling. I was hopeful to have a decision from Judge Roberts by Christmas.

The city's victory dance came to an abrupt halt as there was no doubt that Judge Chapels's opinion and order put a speed bump in the road to summary judgment for them. But the chief would continue to make strategic moves to keep certain officers towing the party line while gaining loyalty from others. It was suspicious that Chief Small awarded promotions to several officers who were in some way involved with my lawsuit, presumably in the event the city would be denied summary judgment and the case would be assigned a trial date.

21
BLACK FRIDAY

While the world seemed to be consumed with *Keeping Up with the Kardashians* and other much-loved reality TV shows, Elsa, without complaint, was fighting cancer for her beloved grandchildren and two sons, Sam, a first sergeant of the South Carolina Army National Guard, and Michael, a solutions architect. God would humble me once again when I volunteered to escort Elsa to one of her chemotherapy treatments the day before Thanksgiving.

When we arrived in the chemotherapy room, much to my surprise, I witnessed many persons—African Americans, Caucasians, Latinos, both men and women—hooked up to IV's with poisonous concoctions dripping into their veins. I thought to myself how unfair it was that these people could not even get a reprieve from the chemo long enough to enjoy a Thanksgiving holiday with their families. And even as the toxic drip saturated the cancer inside their bodies, it was no guarantee any of them would live to see Christmas or any other holiday.

Still emotional from what I had observed in the chemotherapy room, I became furious when I saw many stores open on Thanksgiving Day and more and more people seemingly sacrificing their souls to leave the Thanksgiving dinner table to form human chains in parking lots, while wrapping themselves around the exterior of stores hoping to get the deal of the century. Long before 1863 when President Lincoln declared Thanksgiving a national holiday, pilgrims set the day of Thanksgiving as a way of thanking God for their plentiful harvest. Secular people now mark the Thanksgiving holiday by boasting of their gluttony and having no shame in their idolatry of possessions. I looked at these fanatical shoppers while driving by, and I would become equally affronted when I received a Christmas card from Martha's law firm.

The card informed me that the law firm had foregone their traditional holiday party in lieu of making a ten-thousand-dollar donation to a local food bank. The gracious gesture was all "smoke and mirrors" to me considering Dad and I had already paid thousands of dollars in attorney's fees. After repeated years of monthly legal invoices, I never received the first offer for any *pro-bono* work to be done on my case, all while the severance of my family continued to be most evident during the holidays. The holiday shopping frenzy gave me brief flashbacks of the near riot I experienced on the African mission field, which left me disenchanted.

As with the symbolism of the Thanksgiving holiday, Christ's birth represents the true meaning of Christmas, which has become lost as the holiday became enveloped in commercialism, our need for attainment, and our sense of entitlement. As with past Christmas holidays, ostensibly more value was being placed on what was under the tree than a Savior's birth for the atonement of our sins to save our souls. During Christmas and throughout the year, countless numbers of parents sinfully idolize their children while living out their dreams through them, parallel to the hit TV show *Toddlers and Tiaras*. And closer to home, I desolately witnessed one of my close friends walk a tightrope of veneration with her child helping to mark this year as the year that I was more than ready to pull off the ornaments and pack up the Christmas tree.

Once again, I would ring in the New Year, praying for a trial date to be set while wishing for peace and prosperity for those closest to me. The year 2012 would start out with good news, but after January, I would experience a roller coaster of joy and sorrow over the next few months. My first ray of sunshine occurred when Elsa stopped by and ecstatically reported to me that a scan of her body showed the cancer was regressing and the future was once again optimistic. As we would pray together, she would always pray I would prevail in my lawsuit against the city and I would always pray her cancer would go into full remission and she would be a living tribute for many without hope. More good news came when after months of backbreaking labor, our small congregation pulled together so we could finally move into our new house of worship. It was so remarkable sitting in our newly remodeled sanctuary and listening to our pastor preaching on God's grace and his vision for our church. The pastor repeated scripture:

> *Jesus replied: Love the Lord your God with all your heart and with all your soul and with all your mind. This is the first and greatest commandment.* **(Matthew 22:37–38, NIV)**

Absorbing the pastor's words and taking in the smell of wet paint on the sanctuary walls, I could not help but to begin feeling optimistic and enthusiastic for the future.

February would be an uneventful month, but March 2012, would bring dreadful news when Elsa came to tell me that a newer scan revealed the cancer had grown in other places in her body despite the aggressive treatment her oncologist had prescribed. Over the next several weeks, I would take turns with members of her family driving her to the emergency room at all hours of the day and night because she was vomiting and in excruciating pain. The remedy was always to admit her into the hospital until doctors could stabilize the pain and the vomiting would eventually subside. After several admissions and discharges from the local hospital, Elsa would have to humble herself to be cared for by her immediate family, as well as her parish community. I was disheartened, but I asked Sabina and her family to join me in praying for God's will and that Elsa would not continue to suffer.

I received more unsettling news when Martha called me to inform me that Judge Roberts had ordered a conference call with her and one of the city's attorneys, Kate Thiel. I was outraged to learn that after having Judge Chapels's opinion and order on his desk for the past five months, he was unable to simply review all of the law briefs, all the arguments from both sides, and any documents of evidentiary value that had already been submitted to make his ruling. It was appalling to learn that in the eleventh hour, Judge Roberts decided during the infamous conference call to open up the retaliation points to be further argued by the city's legal team, with a closing rebuttal to be made by Martha. This abracadabra by Judge Roberts gave the city yet another opportunity to reach back into their bag of magic tricks while Judge Roberts resembled the Lance Armstrong of performance-enhancing legal maneuvers.

Throughout the arguments and rebuttals, the city's defense team did their best to deliberately conceal my meeting with the city manager and then presented a half-baked version of my meeting with Chief Small and my complaint to Lieutenant McFarland. Now, the city's knife-wielding legal team could once again combine their law degrees to deviously cut up my written complaint to the SCHAC and my oral complaints of discrimination and retaliation to the city manager and Lieutenant McFarland, in order to feed it back to the court like shark bait. Unfortunately, by then, I was of the opinion that scrutinizing actuality and then writing disproportionate interpretations was how defense attorneys sacrificed their souls. It was what they got paid to do, but I was ready for someone to stick a fork in me because I was done; I was tired of all the legal shenanigans.

It was implausible to me to learn that Judge Roberts steered Martha into arguing a Price-Waterhouse case in her new rebuttal to the court, a case which the Fourth Circuit Court of appeals had interpreted unfavorably for employees, unanimously siding with the employer. After researching the Price-Waterhouse case, I adamantly protested to Martha not to make any reference to Price-Waterhouse in my case as I plainly saw how disadvantageous and irrelevant this conjecture would be for my retaliation claims. Martha concluded that she was abiding by Judge Roberts's instructions, as I questioned how many more Molotov cocktails were going to be thrown at me before I would get an opportunity to present my case before a jury. I stood by scripture as I prayed about how Martha would write her rebuttal to the court. *Remember, it is sin to know what you ought to do and then not do it.* **(James 4:17, NLT)**

I also made Martha fully aware that most of the witnesses in my case were growing wearier of a fractured justice system, which was barely limping along. It had been almost five years since I made my initial complaint and went through all the required legal steps, and within that time, one of my witnesses moved to Utah, while another witness was living in North Carolina; additionally, another witness sacrificed his soul by jumping the fence to play on the city's team after being promoted, and unexpectedly, another witness threw down his cheerleading pompoms and renounced testifying, as another witness began combating challenges from aging. Understandably, the importance I placed on my case was evaporating in the minds of my witnesses as they had no dog in this fight. I had a lot of concerns, but I knew I had many people praying for me as I continued to strengthen my faith through prayer, scripture reading, and church attendance.

There was so much enthusiasm building up to our first Easter Sunday celebration in our new church, and the possibilities for winning souls for Christ seemed endless. But on April 4, 2012, just four days before Easter Sunday, my pastor died of a heart attack at the young age of fifty-three while cutting grass at his home. Although his journey was complete, his untimely death left me devastated and searching for answers as he left behind a wife, three children, and a newly born grandson. As Elsa's health continued to deteriorate, she made a failed attempt to console me over my pastor's death when she told me, "Meeting Jesus is a journey we all will have." She paused and then said, "My day is coming soon."

I knew by these words she had accepted that she was dying, and as I weighed the severity of her words, my nostrils immediately became moist as tears pushed up against the brim of my eyelids. Those words were like the foot of an immovable beast bearing down on my chest, and with one fleeting look, evidence of me being an emotional wreck was about to pour out with a force equivalent to that of Niagara Falls. I quickly gave my best impression of a sneeze to mask my weakness, while complaining that I was having an allergic reaction to something in the air. Elsa gave me a D grade for my theatrical audition but tried to lighten my load with redundant chitchat.

Once I had looked away from Elsa, my neck would no longer turn in her direction, as I was secretly struggling with her condition worsening and I was weighing my own life and how to repair the damage done to my soul. I couldn't deny the truth in Elsa's words: "We are all on a journey to meet Jesus." I choked back tears of dismay and regret. Elsa sensed my need for silence, and tranquility comforted us for the remainder of our evening together.

Often after a hard rain, a cloudy sky will give way to the sun and a rainbow will emerge. I received the appearance of a rainbow through encouraging news from Martha as she informed me that a trial date had been set for September 24, 2012, and jury selection would occur on June 18, 2012. The sequence for these events seemed anomalous since we had not received a recommendation on summary judgment from Judge Roberts and the final opinion from Judge Chapels, but I took the news as a good sign that things were finally headed in the right direction.

22

SUMMARY JUDGMENT

By the end of April 2012, I received Judge Roberts's final report and recommendation, and it would be one more *déjà vu* nightmare for me as he would dismiss my retaliation claims, recommending summary judgment be granted to the city. Judge Roberts whittled down my solid retaliation claims from a huge, deeply rooted oak tree into a toothpick. In a nutshell, based on the city's legal team's synthetic arguments, Judge Roberts concluded my complaint to Lieutenant McFarland and my meetings with Small and Long were not protected activity; more specifically, he cited that I did not use proper vocabulary in my complaint of being supervised by an "officer" of a lower rank as opposed to being supervised by a "male" of a lower rank, and that I made statements when complaining that I was "embarrassed" and "humiliated" instead of I was "discriminated" and "retaliated" against when I was put in the position of being supervised by a male of a lower rank.

Judge Roberts also concluded that I didn't use the grievance hearing forum properly to communicate my discrimination and retaliation claims. Judge Roberts disregarded my contention of the language I used in my complaints of discrimination and retaliation to the city manager and the fact that I was waiting on the city manager to take appropriate action prior to addressing the grievance committee. Judge Roberts additionally scrutinized how I filled out the mandatory forms for the SCHAC. As a layperson, unversed in employment law terminology, I relied upon Martha, as my attorney, and the commissions investigator to discern applicable laws according to my specific discriminatory and retaliatory issues.

I tried to maintain a tranquil disposition knowing my case had already been put on the court docket for a September trial and Judge Chapels could overrule Judge Roberts's recommendation, but I could not overlook the odor of egregious depravity emitting from my lawsuit. I was suspicious that Martha had not been forthright with me concerning the conference call with Judge Roberts and Kate Thiel, one of the city's legal counselors, as the basis for the conference call wasn't passing the smell test. I made an appointment to see Martha on May 2, 2012, to express my concerns and to get answers to some tough questions. The email exchanges between Martha and me to set up this colossal meeting consequentially gave this veteran attorney clues for preparing her fiery plan before my arrival to her law firm as my indignant, contemptuous demeanor inadvertently seeped through my typed communiqué.

It was nauseating to me and beyond belief that since 2010, my legal fees were over sixty thousand dollars and now two years later, her attorney fees were looming in excess of one hundred thousand. With the years that had passed and all the debt of the lawsuit, I still didn't feel as if I was any closer to having my day in court than I was when I filed my original complaint in 2007. I took out a second mortgage on my house and depleted Dad's retirement dreams and had nothing left to give with four months remaining before my trial was set to begin. At the prelude of the meeting, I had diligently prayed to God to give me strength and wisdom when apprising Martha that her legal effort in my case and charges for her professional services appeared surreptitious and I expected answers starting with her explicitly divulging the content of the conference call with Judge Roberts and Kate Thiel.

During my drive to Martha's office, I had a lot of time to pray and reflect on the twists and turns of my lawsuit, but I was truly unprepared for the ambiance I would face as we met in the law firm conference room. The meeting immediately took on a David and Goliath feeling as Martha's demeanor was that of a coiled, venomous snake, lying in wait. Martha adamantly defended how efficiently she worked on my lawsuit, shifting from a manipulative tone to hissing insistently. It felt as if I were talking to the Atlantic Ocean when she condemned me for repeatedly expressing my fears and frustrations as I tearfully and despondently updated her on my continued estranged relationship with my dad and stepmom. Martha attempted to conceal her vindictive persona when she tabled the idea to refer me to another lawyer while disguising the offer as her attempt to find middle ground. I recognized this as a dicey proposition for me as I quickly threw down my slingshot and tried to shield myself for the remainder of the inferno. Stunned by Martha's lack of concern or compassion, I raised the white flag and retreated without getting an elucidation for the conference call or the bottomless money pit that Dad and I had fallen into.

After being raked over hot coals by Martha for what seemed like an eternity because of my audacity in questioning the validity of the conference call and my appeal for a detailed, itemized register for where all the money went, I felt as though I had experienced a taste of what hell was like. Sensing victory, Martha finally ended the torturous meeting, still bound by our attorney–client contract we both had signed several years earlier.

As I stood up, I unexpectedly stumbled while trying to find my mental equilibrium; I used one hand to guide me around the empty conference room chairs and the other hand to grab tissues from a Kleenex box on the conference room table, while I unsuccessfully tried to catch incredulous tears from my face. Martha stood unapologetically to meet me as I rounded the table and then triumphantly showed me the exit doors. I walked out of the law firm completely broken; I then concluded Martha and I were polar opposites and prevailing in this lawsuit rested solely on my narrow shoulders as I had just pulled Martha's veil of titles and certificates from her, to witness her hidden, money-driven, dark side.

Uncontrollable tears blurred my vision as I tried to walk through the law firm lobby and into the parking lot. To navigate the sidewalk, I used a heel-to-toe field sobriety test that I had been taught at the police academy. As I maneuvered the corner with hesitant steps, I attempted to focus on three African-American women walking toward me. Seeing my despair as I used tissues to blow my nose and wipe my tears, they paused long enough for one of them to say, "God bless you, girl."

I acknowledged, "Yes, I need Him too," as I did my best to compose myself and find my car.

I opened my car door and was met with stagnate heat emanating from inside. As the hot air smacked me in the face, I thought to myself, *I just came from hell, and I don't ever want to go back!* I sat down and fumbled to get the car key into the ignition switch and then gripped both hands tightly around the steering wheel as I desperately tried to stop the involuntary quivering of my upper extremities.

I turned the car on, and an unexpected blast of hot air came out of the air vents and again hit me squarely in my face. Frustrated, I forcefully turned off the car and flung the driver's-side door open as beads of sweat began running down my forehead, briefly gathering in my eyebrows before running down my temples attempting to merge with the tears streaming down my cheeks. By this time, my Kleenex had disintegrated from the weeping flood, and the tissue remnants made their way to the car floorboard. I leaned my seat back, closed my eyes, and pushed my aching cranium into the headrest.

As I tried to sift through the dialogue Martha and I just had, an avalanche of thoughts flashed through my mind. I envisioned the defense counsel coming out of the wood-work to sit in the conference room as gleaming spectators while stoking Martha's hot coals, which had been earlier prepared for me and laughing hysterically as popcorn kernels spilled from their bowl. I then had haunting thoughts of Donna's travesty as she redacted her sexual harassment complaint, leaving me holding the bag. I recalled the unsettling, degrading encounters I had had with Chief Small and his abhorrence for me through the unyielding, undue corrective action he administered to me. I also recalled the unjust torment I endured while under Ashley's command and then my anguish as Ashley and Donna finally successfully ousted me as a supervisor in the Street Crimes unit, helping Chief Small sacrifice his soul with my unmerited demotion. And just as prevalent were the feelings of guilt for what this lawsuit had put Dad and my family through. I opened my eyes and simultaneously balled up my right hand and deliberately began violently shaking a white-knuckled fist in the direction of heaven while yelling at God, "*I'm not giving up!*"

I was angry, and I blamed God for the thrashing I endured from Martha. Instead of God equipping me for this meeting with Martha, I felt He had abandoned me as I unknowingly walked into a conference room beat-down armed with a slingshot against a giant. But as I regained my equanimity, I thought to myself, *It's a good thing God is a loving God with patience and a sense of humor,* as even though I felt abandoned at that moment, I knew His Word said that He would never leave or forsake us.

Realizing that I did not have the Erin Brockovich attorney that I sought after but instead a soulless, iniquitous legal representative, I turned my thoughts to my dear ally, Magda. She exultantly told me repeatedly she knew early on, and without a shadow of doubt, she was made to be an attorney. As I reflected on what Martha had put me through and Magda's rapid career advancement at her law firm, I silently prayed that Magda would never betray herself by becoming an attorney who would sacrifice her soul for career advancement and worldly attainment. Feeling dehydrated from the sweat, the tears, and the fist-shaking, I stopped long enough to gulp down a bottomless energy drink before making my way back to Myrtle Beach.

June 13, 2012, just over a month after my unforgettable meeting with Martha, I had a day off from work and was busy running through my chores list when late in the afternoon, I received an email from Martha, which was titled "Summary Judgment Granted." Adrenaline raced through my veins as I began to read Judge Chapels's final order on my iPhone. My knees buckled as I fell to a seated position and tried to brace myself. It was a surreal moment, similar to a single woman staring at a home pregnancy test saying to herself, "What do I do now?" For me, "What do I do now?" was when I realized my trial date had been forfeited with the judge's ruling. I was left with feelings of agony, confusion, skepticism, fear, and emptiness. No relief came from knowing that the judge's decision had just brought this chapter of my life to a close. It was a gut-wrenching feeling, as if I had just run a marathon and collapsed ten yards shy of the finish line.

As the adrenaline seemingly began to melt from my body like snow on a sun-filled day, I placed my finger on my pulse to ensure I hadn't flatlined or that I wasn't having some kind of out-of-body experience. The justice system had failed me, and I surmised that it was easier for Judge Chapels to agree with Judge Roberts's final opinion and recommendation than use the fine-tooth-comb approach to untangle hundreds of pages of legal documents to find the truth of the retaliation I had endured. **Ah-ha moment: Without the conviction of the Holy Spirit, we will always do what is easy instead of what is right.**

After anticipating this moment for so long, I recognized life could change in the blink of an eye, and now I had to decide if I was going to go back to work as if nothing had happened to wait for the other shoe to drop or retire immediately with my 401(k) rollover eligibility. I wanted to leave my law enforcement career on my own terms, not through a forced retirement, because I feared further retaliation now that I was no longer under the umbrella of a federal lawsuit. But after praying for God's direction, I tearfully drove to the retirement headquarters as a police officer knowing I would be driving back retired and unemployed.

While making the two-and-a-half-hour drive to the retirement headquarters, I prayed a lot and reflected on many things. It had always been of great importance to me to complete twenty-five years of consecutive service and to remove the black cloud hanging over my head before officially retiring. I was of the belief that the black cloud would depart from me when I stood before a jury of my peers to give a truthful account of what had happened in my career. It would be hard for me to get past not having my day in court and leaving my job just shy of the twenty-five-year mark. I would have to learn to see twenty-five years as just another number, not that miraculous, now unattainable number that would leave me feeling like a failure.

I empathized with quarterback Peyton Manning, a four-time National Football League Most Valuable Player, who led the Indianapolis Colts to a Super Bowl victory and led his team in other Super Bowl appearances. Peyton made it well known to his fans that he wanted to retire from playing the game he loved as a member of the Indianapolis Colts, but despite his contributions to his beloved team, he was released from his contract in March 2012, after fourteen seasons as their "go-to" man.

Ironically, Peyton's departure from a football team he acclaimed occurred just three months before my forced retirement from a department I once venerated. However, many of Peyton's opponents would not share my sympathy because Peyton was undeniably successful as well as being a millionaire. But it's not always about being famous or rich. I found a quote from Billy Graham to help me accept my current disposition: "Our job in life is not to be successful but to be faithful."

While folding my police uniforms and placing them neatly into a box, I contemplated how I would break this terrible news to my family. I could only pray now that this heartbreak was finally over, Dad and my stepmom would exonerate me of my faults and come to the same decision of forgiveness as I had for those who had sacrificed their souls, making me a martyr. I was ready to cut down the briar patches that had created so many lesions and scars for my family and me. Equally as important, I prayed Dad would proclaim Christ as his personal Savior once he would witness the changes God had made in my life as a result of me having faith in the midst of hardships.

I never returned to the police department from my untimely departure to properly say good-bye to coworkers I truly cared for. Instead, after leaving the retirement headquarters and going home long enough to pack, I met my former supervisor, Vick Dionne, fittingly in a church parking lot and relinquished boxes that contained twenty-four-and-a-half-years' worth of a law enforcement career. As I handed over these boxes one by one, I was overcome by a tsunami of memories…graduating from the police academy, my rookie years, the inclusion of women in law enforcement, working through Hurricane Hugo, the officers who had been killed in the line of duty, the promotions I had received, and then of course the demotion—memories which gave me a nostalgic feeling as I surrendered the last box, denoting the end of my career. I tried to remain strong while slipping my badge and police credentials into Vick's hand, but I had to rely on scripture to sustain me as I unsuccessfully fought back a flood of tears.

For I know the plans I have for you, declares the LORD, plans to prosper you and not to harm you, plans to give you hope and a future. (**Jeremiah 29:11, NIV**)

Punctually, I received my final bill from Martha, a whopping $12,146.28, and then the city threw salt on an open wound when I received notice of a bill of costs totaling $1,442.35, submitted by the city's legal defense team for their portion of disposition fees. I was bewildered as Dad and I had already coughed up over $24,000 for disposition fees back in the summer of 2010, and I thought all the fees associated with these depositions had been paid in full, but after summary judgment was granted, the city took one final jab by petitioning the court to make me responsible to reimburse their sum of administrative costs.

This submitted bill appeared gratuitous to me as I had nothing left but lint in my pocket and the city had a gigantic budget of $152.8 million for the fiscal year 2012–2013. I thought, surely, they could have scraped together enough funds from their existing budget to cover this expense, but instead, the city's legal defense team magnanimously advised that they would not put a judgment against me and would not charge interest on the overdue amount if I would agree to a payment arrangement in a timely manner. Broke, but not ruined, I was comforted when reminded of scripture:

We are pressed on every side by troubles, but we are not crushed and broken. We are perplexed, but we don't give up and quit. We are hunted down, but God never abandons us. We get knocked down, but we get up again and keep going. **(2 Corinthians 4: 8–9, NLT)**

With my wall of buoyancy completely demolished from the lawsuit wrecking ball, I began sorting through the pieces of debris of my life and my career while simultaneously praying God would give me the strength to rebuild.

23

SOUL-SEARCHING

I went to Elsa's house, and my last memory of her with no hair, barely conscious, and emaciated still haunts me. As I took note of her labored breathing, I knew her soul would soon depart her body to meet Jesus in heaven. I clutched her hand and leaned over to whisper to her, "When you get to heaven, introduce yourself to my mom and please continue to be a guardian angel over me; I'm at a crossroads in my life."

On July 3, 2012, while attending Elsa's funeral, I couldn't deny my anguish as I stood with other mourners barely moving my lips in a meager attempt to sing a designated hymn. I was wrestling with understanding why God called my pastor home before finishing his work here on earth, and I was also somewhat embittered remembering the destruction cancer had done to Elsa's body and her suffering during the last few months of her life.

I then realized Elsa's journey had finally ended; she was no longer suffering here on earth, but now living with Jesus for eternity. While mourning at her funeral, I reflected how God used Elsa to help convict me, and in my sorrow, I knew how much I would miss her and how desperately I wanted to tell her, "Thank you," one last time. I shook my head in disgust as I thought what little value we place on human life and even less on our souls until, of course, it's too late.

As I sat, staring at the Catholic priest delivering Elsa's eulogy, I continued to contemplate the adversity God was helping me cope with: the lawsuit against my employer, my estranged relationship with my family, my sinful lifestyle, a difficult and painful foot surgery, my pastor's death, and my law enforcement career ending with the uncertainty of my future. These adversities that I now classify as life lessons caused me to do some solemn soul-searching. The soul-searching process was like an archaeological dig for me. It was a protracted, painstaking progression; it took time for me to excavate and examine the dirt in my life before eventually finding the obscured treasure—my soul, which led to my supposition that the soul is a gift from God that should be valued and guarded, not sacrificed.

As I look back to when I was navigating through all of the legal loopholes, I see I never ceased praying for God's will for my life and the outcome of this lawsuit. I went into this torturous lawsuit indiscriminately and came out feeling like a gullible victim of a convoluted legal system, Bernie Madoff style. I couldn't help but to feel as though these legal proceedings were one big Ponzi scheme, where lawyers got richer and someone was always scratching the other one's back to get something in return. But remarkably, I never questioned God's authority for why summary judgment was awarded to the city and why I never got my day in court, as scripture tells us: *Trust in the LORD with all your heart, and do not lean on your own understanding.* **(Proverbs 3:5, ESV)**

Presumably, God saved me from a number of perils if my case were to have gone to trial: predictably, a half-hearted, lackluster courtroom performance by Martha and a potential jury pool similar to the inept, credulous jurors selected in the Casey Anthony trial, as well as the city's lynch-mob legal defense team's rhetoric and of course, the lengthy number of polished testimonies by the command staff, fueled by Chief Small's guiding anthem and strong aversion to me. Looking back, going to trial and winning the lawsuit would have been seemingly perfect redemption, but I believe God's purpose and my true redemption came as a result of purging my soul. Simply put, it was like taking off my police boots to take new steps in Christ.

Even so, I knew there would still be moments that I would categorize myself with people who obsess over the number they see while standing on the scales or the number of candles on their birthday cake, but I had to pray for God to give me peace and understanding, instead of scrutinizing and regretting why I didn't get the contented ending I had prayed for. I would also have to learn not to fret over what people were going to think of me.

As weeks turned into months since the ending of my law enforcement career, I could feel God's grace as I was experiencing transformation occurring within my soul. It became a pivotal time in my life as my beliefs were distinctly shifting. Retirement gave me a surplus of time to think, pray, reflect, and read God's Word, bringing me to the realization that we live in a modern-day Sodom and Gomorrah, where divorce and adultery are seen as just a part of life, the legalization of marijuana is becoming overwhelmingly popular, idolatry is now a predisposed way of life, and gay is the new normal. And as liberalism for same-sex marriage is embraced, politicians and Supreme Court justices have begun sacrificing their souls by flip-flopping on their position from the traditional biblical definition of marriage between a man and a woman to broadmindedness for gay marriage.

In retrospect, it was hard for me to value my own soul when I did not make a conscious effort to separate myself from my own sinful nature. Further confirmation for my conversion came after reading another quote from Dr. Charles Stanley: "We are either in the process of resisting God's truth or in the process of being shaped and molded by His truth." Without a doubt, God's truth was being chiseled into my soul.

My conviction from God first came through Elsa, and my soul became truly remorseful as I read scripture reassuring me of the necessity of my repentance:

> Let there be tears for the wrong things you have done. Let there be sorrow and deep grief. Let there be sadness instead of laughter, and gloom instead of joy. When you bow down before the Lord and admit your dependence on him, he will lift you up and give you honor. **(James 4:9–10, NLT)**

The new acute awareness for the value of my soul caused me to see my humanness for the precarious choices of my past while awaiting the new course my journey would take, as I began being chauffeured by Christ.

24

SUPERLATIVE SOUL OR NEFARIOUS SOUL

s I continued to exercise my faith, I saw my trust in God becoming measurably stronger, even though I still found myself questioning the strength of my self-assurance muscle when running an endurance race with patience, prayer, and perception for this manuscript. I concede that I struggled tremendously throughout the process of writing this book, as I am not a writer and I never enjoyed reading as an adolescent. Many times, I threw my pen down and turned off my laptop, as I told myself that I could not transpose my police career, my adversities, and my Christian beliefs into a manuscript; it was too painful and too difficult of an undertaking.

Naturally, when embarking on a seemingly impossible task, I would be more conscious of my inability, convincing myself that I could not successfully complete the mission rather than rejoicing in any forward progress I had already made. My insecurity ignited another **ah-ha moment:** Trusting God in every circumstance is essential.

I decided to solicit a free-spirited, suspected agnostic woman named Carly to give her opinion of my memoir before submitting it to a publisher. "It's too preachy!" she declared, while looking at me from across a restaurant table. Carly always had a unique eloquence, causing a yearning in me for an explanation of her words. She then proudly asserted, "I've read the Bible from cover to cover, and I'm an atheist!"

Yikes, I silently thought. As I mulled over her impassive, irreverent frame of mind for God the Father, God the Son, and God the Holy Spirit, I became grief-stricken and tried to hide my bafflement and sorrow with a ravenous appearance, shoveling unprecedented amounts of hummus and flatbread into my mouth.

I was disheartened that nothing in my memoir and Carly's own admirable accomplishment of reading the Bible in its entirety had changed her psyche. Undoubtedly, Satan's deceitful myths had a chokehold on her as she freely played in the devil's workshop. I tried to deflect any appearance of awkwardness from my silence, but as I visualized Carly's soul snarled in Satan's barbwire fence, I heard an imaginary clap of thunder and felt a make-believe tremor of the restaurant floor. The haunting image had me praying that soon Carly would approach God with faith, instead of denial and arm-crossing defiance.

Gauging the conversation as we finished our meal, I sensed Carly had hoped the memoir would read as a grandiose story, chockfull of vengeance for those who showcased their nefarious souls instead of exemplifying a superlative soul during their participation in my lawsuit. Not wanting to be confrontational, I rubbed my face in an attempt to diminish any disapproving wrinkles forming on my forehead, but I refused to proffer up an artificial apology for the religious angle my memoir took on. Though my memoir exposed the culpability of many for their part in my lawsuit, it was never written as payback to anyone; instead, it was worth the expenditure of pain, tears, and labor I endured to document my story, with the optimism of helping others.

I sensed a curious tone in Carly's voice as she asked me a concluding question, "How could you truly forgive all those people for what they did to you?" I stared out the restaurant window as I recalled the day I drove home in my ambiguity, after signing my retirement paperwork. Astoundingly, instead of having a sour grapes attitude over my situation, I felt God had put sunshine in my soul. I smiled as I remembered how I had a profound feeling of peace and thoughts of forgiveness that day—peace for the uncertain direction my life would take and forgiveness for the people who had sacrificed their souls and, in the process, hurt me deeply.

In the time I spent crying infinite tears, I learned each day has 1,440 minutes. I could choose to spend this time nursing a grudge and plotting retribution, or I could choose to forgive, creating healing within my soul. I then remembered someone once said, "Forgiveness is not a feeling; it's a decision." Today, as I continue my spiritual journey, I pray for my former coworkers and all who were involved in my lawsuit, and now more than ever, I will humbly extend the olive branch to each of them, should we meet again.

EPILOGUE

As the 2012 presidential election was momentous to me and the United States, equally significant to me is the statistical information from the United States Census Bureau, estimating that there are over seven billion humans sharing our world today! From a religious slant, I believe God created all corners of our universe and everything in it to include each of us: *The LORD God formed the man from the dust of the ground and breathed into his nostrils the breath of life, and the man became a living being.* **(Genesis 2:7, NIV)** And within every man and woman, regardless of race or ethnicity, I believe God created a soul as a valuable gift to every human being, a soul that unmistakably identifies each person as uniquely as a fingerprint.

Theorizing that we damage the core of our soul through unrepentant sin can cause us to blame God for our inadequacies by incorrectly believing God created us a certain way; however, I found no scriptures to support a hypothesis that God put anything in our DNA that would damage or destroy our soul. I actually found the opposite: *And remember, no one who wants to do wrong should ever say, "God is tempting me." God is never tempted to do wrong, and he never tempts anyone else either.* **(James 1:13, NLT)** Having free will, I believe, whatever we place significance on identifies the anatomy of our soul, and absent from God, we will falter through our journey in life, never receiving God's full blessings for those who know and love Him.

Help for me finding and restoring the value of my soul came from reading God's Word. There is no substitute for the truth in God's Word, as the Bible teaches us: *All Scripture is inspired by God and is useful to teach us what is true and to make us realize what is wrong in our lives. It straightens us out and teaches us to do what is right.* **(2 Timothy 3:16, NLT)** For me, finding my soul by reaching for anything else was just an imitation or a counterfeit; God's Word is an anchor for the soul. And I believe God will prune us for His service if we chose to surrender, and through the power of the Holy Spirit, He allowed me to tell my story by sharing a portion of my continuing journey.

As I petition God for peace, joy, and purpose for my life and seek to serve Him exclusively, I am coaching myself not to try to fit into someone else's skin. Since God gives each of us special abilities, I try to focus on the unique talents God gave to me instead of coveting the exceptional gifts others have been blessed with—just as my eyes, ears, nose, and mouth can each do something exceedingly well, but one does not do the others' work.

Nineteen years after the murder of Major Chief Deputy Spencer Guerry, Becky Lorens took a leap of faith and reentered her chosen profession, when in January 2013, at the age of forty-six, she was hired as a police officer with the Horry County Police Department. To this day, Becky remains close to Spencer Guerry's widow and their two sons.

Me and Becky at her police academy graduation (Class 600) May 31, 2013.

INDEX

AUTHOR BIO

renda M. Christy was born and raised in the small town of Fairmont, West Virginia, which is also the hometown of 1984 gymnastics Olympic gold medalist Mary Lou Retton. Brenda began her policing career in 1987 with the Myrtle Beach Police Department and held the rank of police investigator from 1999 until 2007. She retired from law enforcement in 2012 and lives near Myrtle Beach, South Carolina.

For radio, television, and print interviews and speaking engagements, as well as upcoming book signing events, please visit the author's website at: www.athorninmyside.com.

21033761R00118

Made in the USA
Charleston, SC
06 August 2013